HOWARDS END

E. M. Forster's House of Fiction

TWAYNE'S MASTERWORK STUDIES

Robert Lecker, General Editor

HOWARDS END

E. M. Forster's House of Fiction

Alistair M. Duckworth

TWAYNE PUBLISHERS • NEW YORK
Maxwell Macmillan Canada • Toronto
Maxwell Macmillan International • New York   Oxford   Singapore   Sydney

Twayne's Masterwork Studies No. 93

Howards End: E. M. Forster's House of Fiction
Alistair M. Duckworth

Twayne Publishers   Maxwell Macmillan Canada, Inc.
Macmillan Publishing Company   1200 Eglinton Avenue East
866 Third Avenue   Suite 200
New York, New York 10022   Don Mills, Ontario M3C 3N1

Macmillan Publishing Company is part of the Maxwell Communication Group
of Companies.

Library of Congress Cataloging-in-Publication Data
Duckworth, Alistair M., 1936–
    Howards End / Alistair M. Duckworth.
      p.   cm.—(Twayne's masterworks studies ; no. 93)
    Includes bibliographical references and index.
    ISBN 0-8057-8366-0 :   —ISBN 0-8057-8566-3 (pbk.) :
    1. Forster, E. M. (Edward Morgan), 1879–1970. Howards End.
  I. Title. II. Series.
  PR6011.058H6   1992
  823'.912—dc20   92-1184
                                      CIP

10 9 8 7 6 5 4 3 2 1 (hc)
10 9 8 7 6 5 4 3 2 1 (pb)

Printed in the United States of America

Gentil mia donna, i' veggio
Nel mover de' vostr' occhi un dolce lume

Contents

Illustrations   *ix*
Note on the References and Acknowledgments   *xi*
Note on the Title   *xiii*
Chronology: E. M. Forster's Life and Works   *xv*

LITERARY AND HISTORICAL CONTEXT
    1.   Conflicts of the Edwardian Period   3
    2.   E. M. Forster's Fictional Ways of Knowing   8
    3.   The Critical Fortunes of *Howards End*   12

A READING
    4.   "Work" and "Text"   27
    5.   Plot   41
    6.   Setting   58
    7.   Characters   75
    8.   Conversations   96
    9.   The Narrator   112
   10.   Only Connect . . .   131

Notes and References   *141*
Selected Bibliography   *152*
Index   *159*

Illustrations

E. M. Forster   xiv
Rooksnest and the wych-elm tree   56
Map of Rooksnest garden   57
Manuscript page of *Howards End*   95

Note on the References and Acknowledgments

The standard edition of *Howards End* and most but not all of Forster's other works is the Abinger edition, as cited in the bibliography. Since neither the Abinger edition of *Howards End* nor the Penguin paperback, whose text is that of the Abinger edition, was readily available in the United States when I prepared this study, I used the 1989 Vintage edition as reference text. (In March 1992 the Penguin text was published in the United States by Signet, an imprint of New American Library.) Following the same reasoning, I substituted the Harcourt Brace editions for the Abinger editions of *Aspects of the Novel* and *Two Cheers for Democracy*. The Vintage edition of *Howards End* often differs from the Abinger edition. Where the differences are minor, I have on a few occasions silently cited the Abinger text. Where the differences are substantive, I have noted the fact in endnotes.

I acknowledge with gratitude the cordial help of Michael Halls, who was the modern archivist at King's College Library, Cambridge, during my research visit in July 1990, and the gracious hospitality of Simon Campion, who kindly showed me the garden and meadow at Rooks Nest House (as it is now named), as well as the house's interior. To the provost and scholars of King's College, Cambridge, I am grateful for permission to reproduce the photograph of Rooksnest and the wych-elm tree, Forster's own map of the Rooksnest garden, and manuscript material housed in the Forster collection. To Elizabeth Langland I am grateful for reading this study, and to William Logan and Debora Greger I owe thanks for many kindnesses in Cambridge and Gainesville. I thank the Division of Sponsored Research at the University of Florida for an award which aided my research and the completion of this study. My deepest gratitude is, as always, to my wife, to whom this book is inscribed.

Note on the Title

The original subtitle of this study was *Aspects of the Novel*. As the title of Forster's own work of fictional criticism, *Aspects of the Novel* has an obvious pertinence to the approach adopted in this work, which devotes separate chapters to plot, characters, setting, and so on. But it proved objectionable to the Society of Authors, who believed, with reason perhaps, that it would cause confusion in publication lists and catalogs arranged according to title. I have therefore changed the subtitle to *E. M. Forster's House of Fiction*. This refers to Howards End itself, which is at once a real house (based on Forster's childhood home, Rooksnest) and a metonym—or fictional container of meanings. "House of Fiction" also recalls the phrase Henry James used in his 1908 preface to the New York edition of *The Portrait of the Lady* ("The house of fiction has . . . a number of possible windows not to be reckoned . . . every one of which has been pierced, or is still pierceable, in its vast front, by the need of the individual vision and by the pressure of the individual will."). Since James's views of fiction are invoked in this study both as a comparison and a contrast to Forster's views, the present subtitle seems apropos. Like James's novel, *Howards End* has a human scene (or chosen subject), defined by the kind of window (or literary form) through which it is viewed; as in James's preface, however, neither subject nor form signifies "without the posted presence of the watcher—without . . . the consciousness of the artist."

E. M. Forster
Roger Fry, oil on canvas (1911)

"*Post-Impressionism is at present confined to my lower lip . . . and to my chin, on which soup has apparently dribbled.*"

[Forster's comments on Fry's portrait in progress, in a letter to Florence Barger (24 December 1911).]

Chronology: E. M. Forster's Life and Works

1879	Edward Morgan Forster is born 1 January at 6 Melcombe Place, Dorset Square, London NW1, the only surviving child of Edward Morgan Llewellyn Forster, an architect, and Alice Clara (Lily) Whichelo.
1880	Forster's father dies 30 October.
1883	Forster and his mother move to Rooksnest (the model for Howards End), near Stevenage, Hertfordshire.
1887	Forster's great-aunt, Marianne Thornton, dies, leaving him £8,000; the interest ensures his public school and university education and later gives him the freedom to travel and write.
1890	Attends (unhappily) Kent House, a preparatory (boarding) school at Eastbourne, Sussex.
1893	With his mother, leaves Rooksnest to live in Tonbridge, Kent; becomes a day boy at Tonbridge School (the original of Sawston School in *The Longest Journey*).
1897	Enters King's College, Cambridge, where he reads classics for three years and history for a fourth, obtaining a second class in both subjects. Nathaniel Wedd and Goldsworthy Lowes Dickinson are influential tutors; H. O. Meredith is an intimate friend. In his fourth year Forster is elected to the Apostles, an élite secret society, through which he comes to know G. E. Moore, Lytton Strachey, and Maynard Keynes.
1899–1902	South African (Boer) War.
1901–1902	Departs in October with his mother on a yearlong tour of Italy and Austria. Writes "The Story of a Panic," his first significant work of fiction.
1902	Begins teaching a weekly class in Latin at the Working Men's College in London and lectures on Italian art and history for the Cambridge Local Lectures Board.
1904	Contributes stories to the *Independent Review*, a liberal journal opposing tariff reform and aggressive imperialism. With his

	mother, removes to a house on Monument Green, Weybridge, Surrey, where they remain until 1924.
1905	Goes to Germany for five months as a tutor to the children of Elizabeth, Countess von Arnim-Schlagenthin, at her family estate at Nassenheide, Pomerania. *Where Angels Fear to Tread* is published, to warm reviews.
1906	Becomes the Latin tutor and close friend of Syed Ross Masood, scion of an important Muslim Indian family. Liberal government, with the backing of the Labour party, begins a program of radical social reforms.
1907	*The Longest Journey* is published.
1908	*A Room with a View* (begun in 1903) is published. Begins work in the summer on *Howards End*; in September he goes to Italy for a holiday.
1909	Lloyd George's "people's budget" is rejected by the House of Lords. Imprisoned suffragettes on hunger strike are forcibly fed by prison authorities. Louis Blériot makes the first air crossing of the English Channel. Responding to complaints about the dust caused by motorcars, the Road Board makes money available to tar the highways.
1910	*Howards End* is published on 18 October; at 31, Forster has arrived as a major English novelist. He associates more fully with the Bloomsbury Group, which includes Vanessa Bell, Virginia Stephen (later Woolf), Lytton Strachey, Maynard Keynes, and Roger Fry. Fry organizes the first Post-Impressionist Exhibition, beginning in October. Forster begins *Arctic Summer* (which he would abandon in 1912).
1911	*The Celestial Omnibus*, a collection of six of Forster's short stories (written from 1903 on), is published. *Howards End* and *A Room with a View* are published in the United States.
1912	Visits Forest Reid in Belfast. In October he leaves for a six-month visit to India in the company of G. L. Dickinson and R. C. Trevelyan. Stays with Masood at Aligarh and visits the maharajas of Chhatarpur and Dewas State Senior.
1913	Visits Edward Carpenter at Millthorpe, Derbyshire, and a memorable encounter there with George Merrill inspires him to begin *Maurice*, his novel of homosexual love; completed in its first version in 1914, it would remain unpublished during Forster's lifetime. Begins his Indian novel.
1914–1918	Works as a cataloger at the National Gallery at the outset of the First World War. In early 1915 he and D. H. Lawrence have an intense relationship. In the autumn of 1915 he leaves

England to work for the Red Cross in Alexandria, Egypt, where he meets the Greek poet Constantine Cavafy, whose work he later makes known to an English audience, and Mohammed el Adl, a tram conductor with whom he begins an intimate friendship.

1919–1920   Returns to England and becomes a prolific literary journalist, reviewing for the *Daily Herald*, the *Nation*, the *Athenaeum*, and other journals.

1921   Makes a second extended visit to India in March, as private secretary to the maharaja of Dewas State Senior. In the wake of the 1919 Amritsar massacre, Forster gives a more somber tone to his Indian novel. Second American edition of *Howards End* is published.

1922   Sails from India in January, and in Egypt visits Mohammed El Adl, now in the last stages of consumption. *Alexandria: A History and a Guide* is published in Alexandria. Meets J. R. Ackerley.

1923   Arranges for Ackerley to be appointed private secretary to the maharaja of Chhatarpur. *Pharos and Pharillon*, a collection of essays written in Egypt, is published.

1924   *A Passage to India* is published in England and America, to great acclaim. Begins a correspondence and friendship with T. E. Lawrence. Forster's Aunt Laura dies, willing him the lease on West Hackhurst, Abinger Hammer, Surrey. With his mother, moves there from Weybridge.

1927   Gives the Clark Lectures at Cambridge, published as *Aspects of the Novel*.

1928   *The Eternal Moment*, a collection of six stories written before 1914, is published.

1929   Goes on a cruise to South Africa.

1930   Ackerley introduces Forster to Bob Buckingham, a London policeman, who marries in 1932 but remains Forster's most intimate friend for the rest of his life. On D. H. Lawrence's death, Forster defends his high literary achievement against detractors, including T. S. Eliot. In the tense decade to come, Forster's liberal views, expressed in BBC broadcasts and journalistic pieces, earn him the respect of left-wing writers, such as W. H. Auden and Christopher Isherwood.

1934   Becomes president of the National Council of Civil Liberties (NCCL), founded in protest against police treatment of hunger marchers. Collaborates with Ralph Vaughan Williams on "The

Abinger Pageant." *Goldsworthy Lowes Dickinson* is published.

1935   Gives address, "Liberty in England," before the International Congress of Writers in Paris.

1936–1939   The Spanish Civil War involves many younger writers on the side of the republicans.

1936   *Abinger Harvest*, a collection of some 80 previously published pieces, is published.

1937   Masood and the maharaja of Dewas State Senior die.

1938   Collaborates with Vaughan Williams on *England's Pleasant Land*. Contributes "Two Cheers for Democracy" to the *Nation* (New York), the first essay in a series by various authors entitled "Living Philosophies."

1939–1945   Continues to defend the liberal tradition and to work in behalf of the NCCL during the Second World War. Opposes government attempts to prevent free speech on the BBC and broadcasts regular talks to India.

1941   Penguin issues two printings of *Howards End*, bringing the paperback total to 110,000 copies (further printings of 60,000 and 85,000 are issued in 1943 and 1946, respectively).

1943   Lionel Trilling's *E. M. Forster* is published in the United States; Trilling singles out *Howards End* as Forster's masterpiece.

1944   Presides at the London PEN conference in honor of the tercentenary of Milton's *Areopagitica*.

1945   Forster's mother dies 11 March. From October to December he pays his third and final visit to India and is feted as a famous author and public figure.

1946   On returning to England, he is dismayed to learn that his lease on West Hackhurst will not be renewed. At this time King's College bestows an honorary fellowship on him with an offer of a room in college; he remains in residence for the rest of his life.

1947   Pays his first visit to the United States; at Harvard University, lectures on "The Raison d'Etre of Criticism in the Arts."

1949   On a second visit to the United States, lectures at the American Academy of Arts and Letters on "Art for Art's Sake."

1951   *Two Cheers for Democracy*, a collection of 66 essays, articles, and broadcasts, is published. *Billy Budd*, with music by Benjamin Britten and libretto by Forster and Eric Crosier, premieres at Covent Garden.

Chronology

1953   Queen Elizabeth II makes him a Companion of Honor. *The Hill of Devi*, a selection of his 1912–13 letters from Dewas State Senior, is published.

1956   *Marianne Thornton: A Domestic Biography* is published.

1960   Appears as a defense witness in the *Lady Chatterley's Lover* obscenity case.

1965   A dramatization of *Howards End* is produced at the Arts Theatre, Cambridge. (Revised, the play will be staged in London in 1967; other dramatizations of *Howards End* include radio broadcasts on the BBC Home Service in 1964 and BBC Radio 2 in 1971 and a television dramatization on BBC 1 in 1970.)

1967   J. R. Ackerley dies.

1969   The queen appoints Forster to the Order of Merit.

1970   Forster dies 7 June, aged 91, at the Coventry home of Bob and May Buckingham; his ashes are spread in the garden.

1971   *Maurice* is published.

1972   *The Life to Come*, a collection of 14 stories—most unpublished, more than half on homosexual subjects—is published in the Abinger edition of Forster's works, which begins publication this year.

1977   First volume of P. N. Furbank's biography of Forster is published.

1978   *Commonplace Book* is published. Second volume of Furbank's biography is published.

1983   First volume of *Selected Letters of E. M. Forster* is published.

1984   Film of *A Passage to India*, directed by David Lean, is released.

1985   B. J. Kirkpatrick's *Bibliography* (2d ed.) lists translations of *Howards End* in Arabic, Czech, Finnish, French, German, Hungarian, Italian, Japanese, Norwegian, Polish, and Spanish. Second volume of *Selected Letters* is published.

1986   Film of *A Room with a View*, directed by James Ivory, is released.

1987   Film of *Maurice*, directed by James Ivory, is released.

1992   Film of *Where Angels Fear to Tread*, directed by Charles Sturridge, is released. Film of *Howards End*, directed by James Ivory, is released.

LITERARY AND HISTORICAL CONTEXT

1

Conflicts of the Edwardian Period

Howards End was published on 18 October 1910. E. M. Forster's fourth novel in six years, it established him, at the age of 31, as a major Edwardian novelist, fit to be placed on the same shelf with H. G. Wells, Arnold Bennett, John Galsworthy, and Joseph Conrad. King · Edward VII had died the previous May, shortly after his annual pilgrimage to Biarritz. The king's death marked the end of an era, and Edward's reign—followed quickly by the holocaust of World War I— soon acquired in the eyes of the nostalgic the aspect of a social Eden before the Fall, a time of order and harmony, the golden evening of Empire and the Pax Britannica. Such a retrospect, enshrined in the aristocratic portraits of John Singer Sargent and the country-house paintings of Sir John Lavery, was both flawed and partial: flawed in that it held up as an ideal a life of conspicuous display, requiring battalions of servants for its maintenance; and partial in that it excluded from view the problems of Britain's cities—poverty, ill health, substandard housing—and the growing tension of its relations with Germany.

Far from a paradise, the Edwardian period (1901–10) was a time of social and political strife. Irish nationalists, seeking the home rule that Gladstone had failed to persuade Parliament to approve in the late nineteenth century, were bitterly opposed by Ulster unionists. Organized labor, incensed by the judicial decision in the Taff Vale case (1901), in which a trade union was successfully sued by its railway company employers, demanded remedial legislation and repeatedly struck for better pay and working conditions. Militant suffragettes, pursuing equality at the polls and in the workplace, turned from heckling at political meetings to arson and crimes against property after their imprisoned sisters on hunger strikes were subjected to forcible feeding by the authorities. Meanwhile, the War Office and the Admiralty, perceiving threats in the expansionist policies of post-Bismarckian Germany, committed Britain to a costly armaments race. Against this background, the "life of telegrams and anger" that Forster attributes to the Wilcox men in *Howards End* applied to the political climate of the time, and the novel's epigraph "Only Connect . . ." might well have been addressed to a whole society in which unionists and nationalists, management and labor, men and women, English and Germans, seemed incapable of conciliation.

Divisiveness appeared within as well as between political groups. At the time of the South African War (1899–1902), the Liberal party divided into "little Englanders," who opposed the war, and "imperialists," who supported it. This is the period when Edward Elgar became, effectively, the composer laureate of England. *Pomp and Circumstance, Marches Nos. 1 and 2* dates from 1901 and the *Coronation Ode* of 1902 contains the text of *Land of Hope and Glory* ("Wider still and wider, may thy bounds be set. / God who made thee mighty, make thee mightier yet!"). Elgar's use of march rhythms and an orchestration giving prominence to brass was perfectly suited to the chauvinist mood of an English public uneasily aware of trade rivalry with Germany (and with an inferiority complex anyway concerning German music).[1] The patriotic Mrs. Munt taps her feet to *Pomp and Circumstance* at the Queen's Hall in chapter 5 of *Howards End*, but Margaret Schlegel dislikes the piece, and their German guests politely leave.

Charles Wilcox in *Howards End* brings back a Dutch Bible from the Boer War, and the detail suggests that the Wilcoxes represent those liberal imperialists who, from 1902 to 1905, to the dismay of their traditional free-trade colleagues, made common cause with Joseph Chamberlain, the colonial secretary who in 1903 proposed a policy of tariff reform—a system of protectionist measures that gave preference to goods from the Empire and exacted duties on goods from other trading nations. Tariff reform was not a clear-cut issue, however; a Fabian like George Bernard Shaw was willing to support reform if the revenues were applied to public purposes and not used to reduce taxes on unearned income.[2] It was becoming clear to many progressive liberals that free trade and laissez-faire—the staple doctrines of "classical" liberalism as it had descended from Adam Smith, James Mill, Jeremy Bentham, and David Ricardo—might no longer be sustainable. Since the 1870s, when Americans extended their railroads to the Midwest and began shipping vast quantities of cheap grain across the Atlantic, Britain had suffered from a depression in agriculture. One consequence was a large-scale movement of agricultural laborers to the cities. In *Howards End*, Leonard Bast tells Helen Schlegel that his ancestors lived in Lincolnshire and Shropshire. He himself, "near the abyss" of poverty in London (47), is thus a representative victim of a movement that, as C. F. G. Masterman argued in *The Condition of England* (1909), was leading to the demise of rural England and its yeoman class, to the growth of suburbia, and to the transformation of London into a city of spectator sports, yellow journalism, and frenzied speed and pollution, of which the motorcar was a chief cause and symbol.[3] Masterman was a radical Liberal M.P. for constituencies in East London, and his work of social analysis bears remarkable similarities to Forster's novel.[4]

Conditions in the cities were appalling, as a series of reports, from Seebohm Rowntree's *Poverty: A Study of Town Life* (1901) to Sidney and Beatrice Webb's *Minority Report of the Poor Law Commission* (1909), revealed in detail.[5] In *Howards End* the narrator states, "We are not concerned with the very poor" (47); Forster is here distinguishing his novel from one like Jack London's *The People of the Abyss* (1903), not announcing his disregard for the poverty-stricken lower classes. As a liberal connected back through his father's family to the

Clapham Sect—a group of dissenting philanthropists who fought in the early nineteenth century for the abolition of slavery in the British Empire and for prison reform—Forster was as aware of the need for improvement in the conditions of the poor as he was committed to the traditional liberal ideals of individual freedom and equality of opportunity.[6] Thus he welcomed with enthusiasm the inauguration of the *Independent Review* in October 1903. The magazine opposed Chamberlain's aggressive imperialism and sought sanity in foreign affairs and a constructive policy at home. Goldsworthy Lowes Dickinson, who had been Forster's tutor at King's College, Cambridge, recognized in the opening number that legislation should pursue the traditional liberal aim of giving the utmost scope to individual liberty but that this aim required a "gradual revolution in all the fundamentals of society, law of property, law of contract, law of marriage."[7]

More than a "gradual revolution" was initiated in 1906 after the Liberals, with the aid of the nascent Labour party, won a landslide victory at the polls. Socialism—the word or its cognates appears more than a dozen times in *Howards End*—was now a force to be reckoned with. In the years after 1906 (the years that roughly correspond to the five-year time span of the action in *Howards End*), the government proposed a series of quasi-socialist measures involving old-age pensions, workmen's compensation, the hours and conditions of work, and unemployment and health insurance. Since the revenues to pay for such reforms were to come from, among other measures, increases in death duties and the income tax and from a new supertax on incomes above £3,000, it is not difficult to understand why the House of Lords unwisely rejected Lloyd George's "people's budget." Nor is it hard to understand, in view of the new powers assigned to both central and local government, why many liberals, too, were troubled by the state's impingement on individual freedom.

As Forster was writing *Howards End*, the dilemmas of the Liberal party in the twentieth century were clear: how was it to balance the needs of the state against the rights of the individual, ensure social progress without capitulating to collectivist measures, reconcile old commitments to industry with new parasitic practices of imperial investment, equate ideals of peace with preparations for war? *Howards End* is a subtle and complex response to the conflicts and contradictions of a swiftly changing, increasingly urban world. It is a fictional response, however, and like Forster's later discursive attempts, in hundreds of essays and broadcasts, to understand the liberal crisis in the twentieth century, it offers no programmatic solution.

In "The Challenge of Our Time" (1946), written during the Labour party's sweeping social reforms, Forster recognizes that he belongs to "the fag-end of Victorian liberalism." Praising that liberalism for its benevolence, humanity, respect for individual differences, lack of color prejudice, and commitment to progress, he also recognizes its blindness to the economic basis of his culture: "In came the nice fat dividends, up rose the lofty thoughts, and we did not realise that all the time we were exploiting the poor of our own country and the backward races abroad, and getting bigger profits from our investments than we should." The challenge of the time was "to combine the new economy and the old morality," that is, to accept government planning while retaining a belief in the moral value of individual freedom. But such a goal is easier stated than achieved. Forster could not gainsay the pressing need for housing, but neither could he accept the government's expropriation of the countryside around Rooksnest, the beloved home of his childhood and the model for Howards End; it is "a collison of loyalties."[8] "Combining" the new economy and the old morality in 1946 proved to be as difficult as "connecting" business and culture in 1910. The persistence of Forster's dilemma in his essay should warn us against expecting to find political solutions in the novel. But Forster's identification and exploration of the social problems of his divided world—his fictional ways of knowing that world in *Howards End*—have a remarkable pertinence to the present.

2

E. M. Forster's Fictional Ways
of Knowing

"Only Connect . . ." is the epigraph of *Howards End*, and the punctuation is important. This is an optative, not an imperative construction. It expresses a wish—for the emergence of a just, harmonious, and whole society—and it acknowledges a fact—that the Edwardian world was disconnected at the social, political, economic, cultural, and sexual levels. An exclamation point after "Only Connect" would have implied Forster's confidence in his ability to solve society's problems as he resolves his novel's relationships and themes.[1] The ellipsis points imply an incompleteness in his novel's project, an honest, perhaps even chagrined realization of his novel's limited ability to correct society's problems or improve human life.

What realistic fiction can do—and what *Howards End* does supremely well—is to specify the consequences of a political and historical moment in the lived experiences of men and women who meet, converse, come together, and move apart in particular places over a particular period of time. *Howards End* is not a statistical abstract or a sociological analysis, but the student of Edwardian England can learn a great deal about the period from the range and detail of its cultural specifications. The novel provides us with data about the incomes of professional people and the unearned incomes of bourgeois intellectuals; the Edwardian obsession with sport (golf, cricket, croquet, tennis, shooting, fishing, swimming); the dependence of the middle and upper classes on servants (butlers, cooks, maids, footmen, chauffeurs, gardeners); conservative opposition to feminist and socialist reforms; avant-garde enthusiasm for Richard Wagner, Claude Monet, and Claude Debussy; intellectual reaction against Victorian art and literature; the emergence of the motorcar and its attendant ills (traffic accidents, speed traps, third-party risks, pollution); middle-class prosperity and mobility, evident in luxury London flats and well-appointed houses in the country; threats to rural life and the creation of preservation societies; Germany's economic challenge and the likelihood of war; and so on down to such details as women signaling their independence by smoking cigarettes.

Howards End also has its own fictional ways of knowing society. Like Jane Austen, from whom he learned "the possibilities of domestic humor," Forster was a novelist of manners.[2] He possessed a discriminating eye for the signs of class difference—in styles of garden and house, in modes of deportment and dress, in choice of pets and leisure activities—and a superb ear for a range of speech forms—social and professional, intellectual and vulgar, polite and domestic, male and female, English and foreign. Nor was his fictional epistemology limited to the organs of eye and ear. Touch is a primary means of connection— or nonconnection—in the novel, separating those, like the Schlegel sisters, who can feel and display affection from those, like the public school–educated Wilcox men, who cannot. In a negative form, touch defines Charles Wilcox's repressed aggression, which explodes at the climax of the novel into homicidal violence.

Taste, too, is important in a novel that, true to its domestic focus, describes a variety of meals, ranging from the junk food that Leonard Bast prepares for Jacky in their squalid Camelia Road flat (soup squares, tongue, and pineapple jelly) to the "English" luncheon at Simpson's in the Strand at which Margaret Schlegel, urged on by Henry Wilcox, partakes of saddle of mutton, to the alfresco feast at Evie's wedding—a feast of iced cakes, innumerable sandwiches, coffee, claret cup, and champagne. Food carries the reader from the near proletarian depths of Edwardian England to the plutocratic heights by way of the pseudo-English Simpson's, which nourishes its guests "for imperial purposes" (158). Nor should we forget, in any catalog of meals, the luncheon of cutlets, claret, Apple Charlotte, and coffee that Tibby enjoys in his Oxford lodgings across from Magdalen College while Helen tearfully recounts her efforts in behalf of the Basts.

Finally, smell is not absent; Margaret Schlegel more than once smells "odours from the abyss" of poverty and despair into which Leonard Bast falls after business and culture fail to aid him.

Forster's ways of knowing in *Howards End* are metonymic, which is to say that what exists in abstract form in a Fabian tract or a statistical analysis exists in the novel as an object—a house, a wisp of hay, a bookcase—or as a character embodying an idea through speech or action. As readers, we are caught up in a drama of human experience occurring in real settings and in human time while we are also challenged by Forster's techniques to reconstruct the social, moral, and political meanings that his fiction enacts through action, description, characterization, dialogue, and commentary. Like *Pride and Prejudice* (1813), Forster's novel offers the delights of active interpretation: Why should hay fever be a moral fault in the Wilcox men? What precisely is suspect about Evie Wilcox's rockery in the garden at Howards End, or the alpine plants she places in it? It is amusing that Evie also breeds dogs and gives them the names of little-known Old Testament characters—but why? It is for the reader to say.

In quite remarkable ways, *Howards End* speaks to present issues. Forster's concerns in the first decade of the twentieth century have not vanished in the last, as a sample list of the novel's oppositions makes clear: memories of a communal and rural past versus the experience of a frenetic urban present; an awareness of society's irreversible commitment to technology versus an awareness of technology's destructive ecological effects; cosmopolitan concerns versus local attachments; the world of business versus the world of the intelligentsia; cultured versus popular tastes; an enthusiasm for art versus an enthusiasm for sports; established male power versus emerging female aspirations; a laissez-faire economy versus a poverty-stricken and hopeless underclass.

Readers looking for a reconciliation of these oppositions through the conventional means of a marriage plot are likely to be disappointed by the tentative and limited connections achieved in the novel's conclusion. For some critics, as discussed in the next chapter, the novel's end testifies to the inadequacy of Forster's liberal humanism as a political creed. Such a view overestimates fiction's power to bring about what social and political agencies have failed to achieve: a just and whole society. Forster's novel is not utopian: obviously preferring the liberal-progressive and humanitarian world of the Schlegel sisters to the utilitarian and social Darwinist world of the Wilcox men, it recognizes not only the relative powerlessness of benevolent intellectuals to effect social change, but also their financial complicity in the very system they critique. In the honest self-reflexiveness of its ideological perspective, however, *Howards End* has great heuristic value. We may or may not share Margaret Schlegel's values—"to be humble and kind, to go straight ahead, to love people rather than pity them, to remember the submerged" (76)—but her values invite us to define our own. We may or may not sympathize with liberal humanism as a political creed, but its representation and critique in the novel are worthwhile. Beyond its high value as entertainment, *Howards End* "forsters" thought and discussion (the pun cannot be original).

3

The Critical Fortunes of
Howards End

Three studies are of great help in understanding the critical reception of Forster's work: Philip Gardner's *E. M. Forster: The Critical Heritage* (1973), which reprints early reviews of Forster's works, from *Where Angels Fear to Tread* in 1905 to *Maurice* in 1971; Frederick P. W. McDowell's *E. M. Forster: An Annotated Bibliography of Writings about Him* (1976), which summarizes criticism and scholarship from 1905 to 1975; and B. J. Kirkpatrick's *A Bibliography of E. M. Forster* (1985), which, among other things, provides a record of Forster's fortunes in the marketplace.[1]

Taken together, these studies show that Forster, like other major twentieth-century authors, has received an enormous amount of critical attention, especially from the 1960s onward. McDowell's monumental compilation contains 1,913 entries, of which 465 pertain to *Howards End* and 729 to *A Passage to India*. Between 1960 and 1975, he estimates, upward of 15 books on Forster appeared. If the annual bibliographies of the *Publications of the Modern Language Association* (*PMLA*) are to be believed, at least another 15 books appeared between 1975 and 1988, as well as several hundred articles and chapters in books and dozens of dissertations. Forster scholarships is alive and well not only in Britain and North America but in France, a tribute perhaps to Forster's friendship with Charles Mauron, who translated all five Forster novels, beginning with *A Passage to India* in 1927. In India, *Passage* has long been an object of interest and study. More surprising is the interest Forster has aroused in Japan—a "connection" between East and West that would have delighted him.

Forster criticism follows the general pattern of twentieth-century literary criticism. At first his novels were reviewed by journalists, men (and women) of letters, and fellow authors. Later they received the attention of academic scholars and critics. Still later his novels have been scrutinized by interpreters suspicious of their political values and formal properties. Such a scheme, of course, needs immediate qualification. Forster's liberalism has been analyzed from the beginning; his fiction to this day attracts good criticism of a historical and formal kind; and journalists interested in Forster's homosexuality, or in the films recently made of his novels, have retained a keen interest in him. For purposes of survey, however, Forster criticism may be divided into three stages: criticism as appreciation, criticism as recovery, and criticism as suspicion.

CRITICISM AS APPRECIATION

The first reviews of *Howards End* in the autumn of 1910 are remarkable for their insight. Forster, it was generally recognized, had arrived. "There is no doubt about it whatever," wrote the reviewer for the *Daily Telegraph*, "Mr. E. M. Forster is one of the great novelists." Taken with its three predecessors, declared the *Athenaeum*'s critic, *Howards End* "assures its author a place amongst the handful of living writers who count." R. A. Scott-James in the *Daily News* described the method of the novel as "a sort of bridge between that of Mr. Conrad and that of Mr. Galsworthy." The *World* reviewer rather deplored the preference given to *Howards End* over Arnold Bennett's *Clayhanger*, also published in 1910, but nevertheless recognized that Forster's novel had been a sensation of the autumn season. Arnold

Bennett himself, writing as "Jacob Tonson," stated that "no novel for very many years has been so discussed by the *élite*."[2]

While almost uniformly laudatory, the early reviews were not uncritical. Several reviewers found the ending unsatisfactory, or were troubled by the improbability of Helen's sexual encounter with Leonard Bast, or by the contrived management of Leonard's death. Others were critical of the characterization: to the reviewer in the *Westminster Gazette*, Mrs. Wilcox represented "a sort of over-soul" for whose significance the reader was inadequately prepared. The *World* critic found Forster one-sided in his sympathies—a modern intellectual who, in the Wilcox men, unfairly represented those who had made England great.[3]

As a general rule, however, fault finding was contained within appreciation. Nothing in the early reviews approaches the sarcasm of Katherine Mansfield's 1917 journal entry: "I can never be perfectly certain whether Helen was got with child by Leonard Bast or by his fatal forgotten umbrella." Instead, the early reviewers praised Forster's humor, his gift for dialogue, his powers of social criticism, and his evocation of place. For R. A. Scott-James, Howards End was both a home (the repository of spiritual values) and a house (a piece of real property); if the literary Schlegel sisters are better heirs than the materialistic Wilcoxes, Forster reminds us that money lies at the basis of poetry, too. As one might expect, the novel's epigraph elicited commentary. The *Daily Graphic's* reviewer, for example, found that the novel connects the world of culture, art, and spirit with that of action, business, and work. Only the *Morning Post* reviewer took the epigraph as an occasion for wit: "We played with the freakish idea that the words were addressed to a dilatory municipal department that refused the benefits of electricity to a house that was wired and waiting."[4]

The early criticism raked much of the ground that later critics would till more deeply. Even the mistake of the *Chicago Tribune's* reviewer—who believed that the author of *Howards End* must be a woman[5]—now seems prescient: not only did it accord with a general appreciation of Forster's treatment of Margaret and Helen, but it also anticipated later interpretations of the novel's androgynous vision.

Of the appreciations of Forster by fellow writers, Virginia Woolf's 1927 article in the *Atlantic Monthly* is the most interesting. Woolf's central proposal concerned the duality of Forster's novels: she characterized him as not only a social observer but a novelist interested in the soul. Like Ibsen, he attempts to combine realism and mysticism but does not quite succeed; what should be the components of a single vision in the novels remains unfused, though Forster almost succeeds, in *A Passage to India*, in animating a "dense, compact body of observation with a spiritual light." Like *Passage, Howards End* was a "large book," and Woolf praised it for its characters, structure, atmosphere, moral discrimination, comedy, and social observation. All the qualities needed to make a masterpiece were there "in solution," but Woolf was disturbed by the novel's didacticism: "We are tapped on the shoulder. We are to notice this, to take heed of that. Margaret or Helen, we are made to understand, is not speaking simply as herself; her words have another and a larger intention."[6]

Woolf's criticism is cogent but not disinterested. An intensely competitive writer, she respected Forster as a critic (indeed as the best critic of her own work) but saw him, as she also saw Katherine Mansfield, as a rival. Thus she was critical of his *Aspects of the Novel* (1927) in her review for the *Nation* (12 November 1927). She disagreed with both his fictional practice and theory, seeing them as a challenge to the high aesthetic idea that she, following Henry James, had of the novel's destiny. What chiefly bothered her was his commitment to "life," a commitment that led him in *Aspects* to disparage James and praise H. G. Wells. In her own fictional manifesto, *Mr. Bennett and Mrs. Brown* (1924), Woolf lumps Wells's novels together with those of the other Edwardian "materialists," John Galsworthy and Arnold Bennett, as examples of how fiction should not be written. In reviewing Forster, therefore, she was defending her own preference for the novel as a form of art rather than a mirror of life. In return, Forster, even while eulogizing Woolf in his Rede lecture of 1941, delivered in the Senate House, Cambridge, restated the criteria of *Aspects*: Woolf, he declared, was incapable of lifelike characterization in the manner of Jane Austen, George Eliot, and—unkindest cut of all—Arnold Bennett.[7]

CRITICISM AS RECOVERY

Even before Lionel Trilling's 1943 study, a more strenuous, academic criticism of Forster had appeared in, for example, the articles of I. A. Richards and of F. R. Leavis. But Trilling's *E. M. Forster*, as just about everyone agrees, is the single most significant work in the history of Forster criticism. Appearing in the middle of the Second World War, the book made momentous claims for Forster's importance and lauded *Howards End* as, "undoubtedly," his masterpiece.

In a sense, Trilling's study—brief, Olympian in its judgments, sparing in its scholarly apparatus—remains a work of appreciative criticism. But his nuanced recovery of Forster's place in a cultural tradition comprising romantic as well as liberal elements carried immense academic authority; no other book on Forster would appear until 1957. In the short run, Trilling made Forster a major author in the United States. In the longer run, his study influenced the excellent historical scholarship of the 1960s and the studies of the 1970s and 1980s, which extended and refined that scholarship.

Trilling was interested in the ways in which Forster, a liberal, was "deeply at odds with the liberal mind." Forster was liberal in his critique of the middle class, soldiers, bureaucrats, the British Empire, business, public schools; equally liberal in his affirmation of spontaneity, sexual fulfillment, and intelligence. Where he departed from liberalism, in Trilling's view, was in his refusal to believe in any easy separability of good and evil. Like Hawthorne, Forster had an unremitting concern with "moral realism, which is not the awareness of morality itself but of the contradictions, paradoxes and dangers of living the moral life."[8] Trilling's "moral realism," like Keats's "negative capability," implies an author who (Woolf's arguments notwithstanding) suspends or complicates his social and moral judgments.

On *Howards End* Trilling is brilliant, tossing off aperçus by the dozen. His most famous remarks treat *Howards End* as a novel about England's fate, with the house symbolizing England itself. But what may be stressed here is the cultural range of Trilling's references. "*Howards End*," he writes, "stands with *Our Mutual Friend* and *The*

Princess Casamassima as one of the great comments on the class struggle." In a discussion of Mr. Wilcox he refers to Plato's *Republic*; Mrs. Wilcox recalls the countess of *All's Well That Ends Well*, as well as Chaucer's patient Griselda; Margaret and Helen, he claims (though Forster disagreed), have the names of the heroines in the two parts of Goethe's *Faust*; and Leonard Bast's child is the Euphorion. Elsewhere in the chapter we read of Montaigne, Erasmus, Milton, and Matthew Arnold. It is easy to see that Trilling had discovered in Forster the values he himself endorsed, particularly the dialogue with great books that contemporary American literature, in his view, lacked. Yet Trilling also saw in *Howards End* the dilemma of the intellectual—the person distinguished, on the one hand, by participation in the historically recent "politics of conscious altruism," but fated, on the other, by the barrier of "articulateness" that separates him or her from both the masses and the middle classes.[9]

The decade of the 1960s was a banner time for Forster scholarship. Since Trilling's book, Forster had produced *Two Cheers for Democracy* (1951), *The Hill of Devi* (1953), and *Marianne Thornton* (1956). These works proved of great relevance to scholars investigating the intellectual backgrounds to Forster's fiction. So, too, did Noel Annan's magisterial study of Leslie Stephen (father of Virginia Woolf). Frederick C. Crews, turning a Princeton Ph.D. dissertation into *E. M. Forster: The Perils of Humanism* (1962), produced what remains one of the best books on Forster. And Wilfred Stone, after eight years of research, which included conversations with Forster and some of his Cambridge and Bloomsbury friends, published *The Cave and the Mountain* (1966), a work of comprehensive erudition.[10]

These and other 1960s studies demonstrate that Forster was not simply a "liberal" writer; he also belonged, as John Beer argues, to the romantic tradition of Blake, Coleridge, and Shelley.[11] In H. A. Smith's terms, he spoke in two voices: the voices of intelligence, culture, and reason, on the one hand, and of instinct, nature, and religious insight, on the other.[12] For Stone, he pursued in fictional ways John Stuart Mill's goal of reconciling the analytic temperament of the Enlightenment with the synthesizing imagination of the Romantic period.

Or like Matthew Arnold, he held up the light of culture against the forces of selfishness and materialism, calling society in the process to an awareness of its best self. In Stone's view, *Howards End* could be read as "the most explicit test of Arnold's notion of culture in our literature."[13]

The great value of these works lies in their scholarly recovery of the intellectual contexts that inform Forster's thought and art: the Clapham Sect, from whom he derived a social conscience if not their Christian faith; the writings of Coleridge, Bentham, and such Victorian "sages" as John Ruskin and Matthew Arnold, whose mantle, in curious Edwardian ways, he wore; Cambridge in its brilliant period at the turn of the century, when J. M. E. McTaggart, the idealist philosopher, and Nathaniel Wedd and Goldsworthy Lowes Dickinson, his tutors at King's College, were of more influence than the Bertrand Russell of *Principia Mathematica* (1910) or the G.E. Moore of *Principia Ethica* (1903); the Bloomsbury Group—including Virginia and Vanessa Stephen, Clive Bell, Lytton Strachey, Maynard Keynes, and Roger Fry— in whose company, though he remained very much "the elusive colt of a dark horse,"[14] Forster would have encountered once more the Moorean faith in the "good," defined in terms of complex wholes of consciousness that derive from an intense perception of beauty in art or nature, or from personal relationships.

Heirs of Trilling as they were, these scholars were not always subservient sons. In Crews's study, Trilling's view of Forster's "moral realism" has become a sense of Forster's "tragic irony," and the "plot" of his interpretation is one in which Forster's humanistic faith in reason and progress is eroded and replaced by a darker vision of humans' impermanence in nature. In this scheme, *A Passage to India* becomes Forster's "sole claim on posterity" (178); and *Howards End*, far from being a masterpiece, is demoted to the status of a failed attempt to ensure the survival of liberalism.[15] Stone's view of the novel is even harsher. Unimpressed by Forster's "relinquishment" of the hero role to the women in the novel, he argues that "Forster's fictional transvestism does not increase our confidence that he will be an impartial mediator between Red-Bloods and Mollycoddles."[16] Like Crews, he discovers nihilistic implications in *Howards End* and severely concludes: "The malignancy inherent in a spiritual-esthetic withdrawal is a subject Forster knows well. . . . But in fictionalizing the problem, he has presented a moral failure as a triumph—and, in the name of much that is beautiful and fine, has become the partisan of much that is sick and corrupt."[17]

CRITICISM AS SUSPICION

Forster's reputation at his death in 1970 remained high. Though he had not published a novel for 46 years, his essays and broadcasts—and latterly, the significant criticism he had received—had kept him in the public mind as a humanist and a sage. In 1969 he had received the Order of Merit; some believed he deserved the Nobel Prize. He remained in the public eye with the posthumous publication of *Maurice* (1971), his novel of homosexual love, and *The Life to Come* (1972), a collection of short stories more than half of which had homosexual content. A little later appeared P. N. Furbank's authorized biography (1977, 1978), Forster's *Commonplace Book* (facsimile edition, 1978), and the selected letters (1983, 1985). Meanwhile, standard editions of his works were published in the Abinger edition, under the editorship of Oliver Stallybrass, and in another medium, David Lean's film of *A Passage to India* (1984) and James Ivory's films of *A Room with a View* (1986) and *Maurice* (1987) exposed Forster's works to a wide audience.

Observing the huge body of Forster criticism, Alan Wilde remarked in 1985 that Forster "called forth and controlled precisely the kind of criticism he has received."[18] Generalization is suspect regarding recent studies as various as those by John Colmer, John Sayre Martin, Glen Cavaliero, Claude Summers, Christopher Gillie, and Norman Page; but their findings tend to confirm or refine rather than radically alter received interpretations of Forster's novels. *Howards End* is the exception only in that it has been resurrected from the low estimation in which it was held by Crews and Stone; if it has not regained the status given it by Trilling as Forster's masterpiece, it has usually been coupled with *A Passage to India*—as it was by Woolf—as one of Forster's two major novels. As for the posthumous works, Forster scholars, while not always agreeing on the instrinsic value of *Maurice* and *The Life to Come*, have resisted arguments that these works lower Forster's literary status.

Such arguments were often accompanied by a suspicion of or hostility to Forster's homosexuality. Samuel Hynes, for example, argued in *Edwardian Occasions* that Forster's homosexuality as such was not the critic's business, but that the homosexuality of his imagination was another matter; it did affect the novels, most obviously in Forster's failure to imagine in convincing ways heterosexual relations and marriage itself. For Cynthia Ozick, Forster's liberal views in the major novels were devalued by the appearance and the subject of *Maurice*. For Denis Altman, Forster's position was compromised by the socially induced guilt that led him to accept social opprobrium as a given and to seek freedom for homosexuals only in escape or fantasy. For some gay liberationists, insensitive surely to the pressures of English history, Forster's refusal to come out of the closet in his lifetime was reprehensible. For Joseph Epstein, Forster's novels were "chiefly screens for their author's yearning for freedom for his own trapped instinctual life."[19]

Feminist criticism could be equally reductive. Jane Marcus was upset by Forster's obituary comments on Virginia Woolf's feminism and his depreciation of Woolf's *Three Guineas* (1938).[20] Others, observing the harsh treatment of women in *Maurice*, were reminded of the misogynism in the previous novels, especially in the characterizations of Agnes Pembroke and Mrs. Failing in *The Longest Journey* (1907). Patricia Stubbs recognized that Margaret and Helen in *Howards End* are feminists but judged the novel to be deficient because it failed to represent women at work and accepted "the traditionally rigid separation between male and female psychological characteristics."[21]

Feminist criticism of another persuasion, however, could find great value in Forster's fiction. In *Forster's Women* (1975), Bonnie Finkelstein discovered an androgynous vision in *Howards End* and also noted the antifeminist character of readings that assume Henry Wilcox to be gelded at the end. Elizabeth Langland agreed that Forster purchased sympathy for the female point of view and exposed the grounds of patriarchal ideology, but argued that Margaret Schlegel is neither the conventional female discovered by Stubbs nor a harbinger of androgyny; instead, she retains her difference as a woman while escaping from social constructions of the feminine and the maternal.[22]

What has given vigor to much recent criticism, then, are disagreements on the question of Forster's sexual politics. In Peter Widdowson's *E. M. Forster's "Howards End": Fiction as History* (1977), Forster's politics, *tout court*, are once again the object of powerful—and suspicious—analysis. Widdowson is critical of liberalism for failing to recognize that the democratic reforms it won in the nineteenth century—reforms that did not extend to female suffrage—were made in the interests of the capitalist middle class, which was intent on profit and the acquisition of property. Widdowson recognizes that Forster was aware of liberalism's limitations, but gives *Howards End* a negative value when he equates the achievement of the novel with its inability to accommodate liberal values in its form: "The rich ambiguity, the fundamental *irresolution* of *Howards End* are key factors in its importance as a novel."[23]

Widdowson tries to walk the fine line between praise and blame, but in faulting Forster for what he excluded from his vision of England—London and the poor—he tends more to the negative. He is critical of Forster's elegiac tributes to the English countryside for their lack of a basis in contemporary history (four-fifths of England's population was urban as Masterman pointed out in 1909). Most of all, Widdowson criticizes the contrivances of Forster's plot, by means of which Forster repelled the social elements that endangered his vision: "Leonard has to die to clear the way for his son to be 'Liberal England's' heir untrammelled by the drab reality of his father's life and class."[24]

Widdowson's study gains its power not from its novelty—others have argued that Forster imposes a vision on recalcitrant facts—but from its political conviction: he is in no two minds about the political

infeasibility of moral individualism or the necessity for radical economic reform as the precondition of cultural improvement for a whole
community. To Forster, who was in two minds on these matters,
Widdowson therefore responds captiously, tending to stress what is
not achieved or included rather than to appreciate what is. In *Fiction
as History*, he compares *Howards End* with Masterman's *The Condition of England*; in an important recent article, he and Peter Brooker
compare the novel to works by D. H. Lawrence, John Galsworthy,
H. G. Wells, George Bernard Shaw, and Constance Holme.[25] If one
consequence of Widdowson's analysis is to make us freshly aware of
Forster's place in a materialist Edwardian context, another may be to
make us more sympathetic to Forster's attempts to connect the fragments of a politically fragmented world. For no Edwardian writer, on
Widdowson's reckoning, achieved an aesthetic vision commensurate
with the political problems of the time. The Fabian Shaw showed in
Major Barbara (1905) that "capitalism is, contrary to the Fabian
programme, the reverse of permeable."[26] In *Tono-Bungay* (1909),
Wells's technocratic utopianism, vulnerable in itself as an ideology, is
compromised by a lingering affection for the neofeudal arrangements
represented in the country house Bladesover. Galsworthy's critique of
the plutocracy in *The Country House* (1907) is not counteracted by a
convincing affirmation of traditional landed life; even if it were, as in
Holme's *The Lonely Plough* (1914), a coherence of vision would be
achieved only at the cost of its anachronism.

CONCLUSION

Widdowson's reading of *Howards End* raises the critical problem of
aesthetic form in relation to belief. In the 1960s, when formalism was
dominant in the academy, scholars tended to equate aesthetic success
with a novelist's ability to synthesize elements of plot, character,
theme, and imagery. Thus Crews, in 1962, preferred *A Passage to
India* to *Howards End* because its "resources of plot and symbolism
work in harmony toward a single end." That single end entails a

realization on Forster's part of "the destructive ironies of his humanism" in *Howards End* and a movement away from "the fashionable slogans of sexual equality, self-expression, and even social responsibility" and toward a vision that placed him among "those great writers who have looked steadily, with humor and compassion, at the permanent ironies of the human condition."[27]

Such a vision now seems problematic: are we really to prefer this Sophoclean wisdom to the humanism, however flawed, that seeks connections within a specific social and historical world, where the ironies, though they may not be "permanent," are sufficiently keen, and the slogans, though they may be "fashionable," are worthy of support or debate? Widdowson would surely say no; different as his politico-evaluative approach is from a 1960s criticism, which assumes a universal human nature, he yet seems to share with that criticism an idealist view of form: Forster got it wrong in *Howards End*, but he could have got it right (or rather "left"?).

What would getting it right mean? When Raymond Williams in *The Country and the City* (1973) indicates a preference for Lewis Grassic Gibbon's *A Scots Quair* (1950) over the novels of D. H. Lawrence, on the grounds that the former work enacts the possibility of social reform through political rather than apocalyptic means, the argument seems forced.[28] Rather than hold novels against a standard in which fictional form and political vision coincide, it may be more useful to accept that all great novels are ideologically problematic, filled with discontinuities, false directions, and internal contradictions. Critics have realized this from the first publication of *Howard End*; like Widdowson, they have for the most part judged it a great novel. Why? Not because it achieves a coherent vision—it does not. Even if it did, that vision would not please all interpreters. *Howards End* is a great novel for other reasons: it provides us with a detailed representation of a world in fragments as this world is experienced in domestic relations and contexts; and through its actions and characters, its dialogues and commentaries, it offers us a variety of perspectives on this world. Some of these perspectives are preferred to others, but none of them—not even that of the much maligned liberal humanist—is isolable as the dominant perspective in whose service the plot enacts (or tries and fails to enact) a political program. *Howards End* is anything but dogmatic and doctrinaire; on the contrary, it is dialogical, inviting its readers to engage its multiple propositions. If it is a classic, it is so in Frank Kermode's and not the usual sense: rather than embodying transhistorical values in harmonious fictional form, or—equally improbably—giving fictional shape to an unexceptionable politics, it offers a plurality of significances that allow for a range of interpretative responses.[29] In the reading that follows I shall be proceeding on this assumption—an assumption that entails, first, a consideration of the formal and generic identity of *Howards End*.

A READING

4

"Work" and "Text"

Howards End my best novel and approaching a good novel. Very elaborate and all pervading plot that is seldom tiresome or forced, range of characters, social sense, wit, wisdom, colour.

—*Commonplace Book* (203)

As Forster's 1958 appraisal suggests, *Howards End* is a classic novel, displaying Forster's skills as a contriver of plot, a portrayer of character, an orchestrator of themes and motifs, a writer of dialogue, and a creator of recurrent and cumulatively meaningful imagery. His skills in these Aristotelian departments account for the excellent close readings his novels have elicited from "practical," "new," and "neo-Aristotelian" critics; those skills may still be appreciated by readers and explicated by critics. Whether considered in terms of its carefully designed structure or its complex verbal texture, *Howards End* is central to what formalist critics in search of organic unity once took—and sometimes still take—a "novel" to be.

Critical explorations in recent decades, however, have altered our ideas of what a novel is, and the fictional qualities that critics took to be central in a climate of neo-Jamesian and neo-Aristotelian orthodoxy no longer command the assent they once did. Russian formalists, such as Viktor Shklovsky and Boris Eichenbaum, who long ago stressed fiction's power to "defamiliarize" objects of perception even as it exposes its techniques to the viewer's gaze, have proved influential in novel criticism. So too has the French semiologist Roland Barthes, who urged a shift in the critical focus from "work" to "text," that is, from a view of the novel as a unique aesthetic product to a view of the novel as an assemblage of narrative structures already present in language or the literary tradition. More recently, Mikhail Bakhtin, the most anti-Aristotelian of all, has defined the novel as a hybrid form comprising many genres and languages and resisting the critical discovery of a unified final form or the isolation of a single authoritative voice.[1]

Different as these theorists are, they share an unwillingness to view the novel as an aesthetic whole in which the component parts of plot, character, theme, and imagery interact in dynamic ways to produce determinate rhetorical effects. Instead, they invite us as readers to enter into a new kind of dialogue with the fictional text. Freed of the idea that a successful novel must be an internally coherent work, propelling its meanings to a decipherable final vision, we may appreciate *Howards End* not, certainly, for its "incoherence" but for its generic diversity, its incorporation of multiple discourses, its "intertextual" relations, and the range of its—often detachable—topics and issues. As we do this, however, we need to register the ways in which *Howards End* as a novel and Forster as a theorist of the novel resist—as well as invite—a "textual" reading strategy.

In obvious ways *Howards End* is a realistic "work." Forster wants us to believe in his characters and their world. Like Henry James, for example, he gives his characters realistic names rather than (as Trollope did to James's disgust) giving them silly names like Dr. Fillgrave or Mr. Quiverfull (who has 14 children). Moreover, even as Forster disputes James's doctrine about point of view, he does not dispute the need to "bounce the reader into accepting what he says."[2] The technical means of the two authors may differ, but their mimetic ends are, it would seem, the same.

In other ways, *Howards End* has realistic goals. Unlike *A Room with a View*, for example, *Howards End* has no elaborate paratextual apparatus; that is to say, its 44 chapters are not divided into parts, nor do they have titles like chapter 6 of part 1 of *Room*—"The Reverend Arthur Beebe, the Reverend Cuthbert Eager, Mr. Emerson, Mr. George Emerson, Miss Eleanor Lavish, Miss Charlotte Bartlett, and

Miss Lucy Honeychurch Drive Out in Carriages to See a View; Italians Drive Them." In fact, they have no titles at all; when Putnam's, without Forster's approval, supplied chapter titles and running heads for the first American edition (published January 1911), he objected, and the offending alterations were deleted in the second (or possibly the third) printing.[3]

Howards End does not, then, deliberately expose its artifice; though Forster does not get rid of chapters entirely, as Woolf does in *Mrs. Dalloway* (1925), he would seem to minimize their capacity to obstruct the reader's belief in his represented world. It would be hard to argue that *Howards End* is a postmodern or postrealist text, employing metafictional means to question its own representational claims. *Howards End* continues to provide readers with the pleasures of the "work," including a fully realized social world, complex ("round") characters, credible incidents, realistic conversations, and, not least, a good story (we want to know what happens next).

All this may be affirmed without injury, however, to the argument that the novel also provides us today with the pleasures of the "text," pleasures that include a recognition of the novel's artificial character and of the seams connecting the multiple discourses that make up its hybrid form. We have only, for example, to consider the famous opening of *Howards End* in its textual aspects:

I

ONE may as well begin with Helen's letters to her sister.

> *Howards End,*
> *Tuesday.*

Dearest Meg,
> *It isn't going to be what we expected. It is old and little, and altogether delightful—red brick.*[4]

Viewed in one way, this is indeed realistic. Like Samuel Richardson's Pamela or Clarissa, Helen "writes to the moment"—in the present tense, on a specific day, and from a specific place. We are given almost immediate access to the expression of a vital personality. Almost immediate: for Helen's letter is introduced by someone else ("one"), who may be an editor or a narrator, we cannot yet say, but who in any case exists on a different ontological level than the character. His or her difference is indicated typographically. Why? Why, for that matter, are all three letters of the first word in the novel capitalized? The answer to these questions may simply be that it was the house style of the publisher. The Abinger text does not capitalize the three letters of *One*, and though it separates the narrative discourse from the epistolary discourse by using different types, it does not italicize the latter. Granting an editorial rationale for using italics (a decision also made by the editor of the Vintage text), we might assume that "one" plays a narrative role (indicated by regular type), whereas Helen plays a dramatic role (indicated by italic type). But such differential typography as easily works against as in the interests of realism. Moreover, the text is preceded by the chapter number—whether Roman or Arabic and whether preceded or not by the word *chapter*—and this, though not as obviously as the titles in *Room*, nevertheless decisively declares the hand of art. Finally, preceding the chapter number is the title page with the paratextual epigraph. I do not wish to belabor this kind of analysis, merely to point out that as we engage in the close reading that both the first sentence of the chapter and the first sentence of the letter richly invite, we may also be observing how the fictional apparatus inevitably declares the artificial, rather than simply representational, character of the fiction.

A similar duality is likely to attend our interpretation of characters' names. For the most part, as noted above, Forster observed the Jamesian doctrine of onomastic decorum. True, "Bast" (rather too obviously implying bastard) verges on the allegorical; but readers who find phallic signifiers in the two syllables of "Wilcox" do so at their own risk. What about "Schlegel," surely a strange name for English girls? Forster's aesthetic task was to exploit the name's allusive potential while, in more than one sense, naturalizing it as a real name. Schlegel alludes to the von Schlegel brothers, the German romantic writers of literature, criticism, and philosophy. An unused passage from a manuscript draft makes the intention clear: the father of the

Schlegels in the novel had been "a distant relation of the great critic," and the allusion works to intensify our sense of Helen and Margaret's idealism, their love of art, music, and the life of the mind.[5]

Forster naturalizes the name in chapter 4 when, after the drama of Helen's visit to Howards End and of Mrs. Munt's rescue attempt, the novel settles for a while at Wickham Place and the narrator has leisure to fill in the background of the three parentless Schlegel children. We learn that the father was a German, a soldier who had fought bravely against Denmark, Austria, and France but had moved to England after the battle of Sedan and the siege of Paris in 1870, disgusted with the imperialist turn Germany had taken under Bismarck. He was the product of a better Germany, the idealistic Germany of musicians, poets, and philosophers, once nourished by small German courts like Esterház and Weimar. His hope was that "the clouds of materialism obscuring the Fatherland would part in time, and the mild intellectual light re-emerge" (30); after his marriage, when his German nephew came to England, he could be bluntly critical of the latter's chauvinistic commitment to a Germany that had forsaken the imagination and the intellect in pursuit of commercial and utilitarian ends.

Ernst Schlegel had married "Poor Emily (or Die Engländerin as the case may be)" (29). Interestingly, in a manuscript draft for chapter 11, Forster had given the mother both a maiden name and a heritage that would have explained the source of the unearned incomes of Margaret, Helen, and Tibby: Charles Wilcox, incredulous that his mother should have bequeathed Howards End to Margaret Schlegel, observes that Margaret is not poor, her mother having been a Pryce, "one of the pottery people."[6] It is a nice detail that could well have remained in the novel.

How well Forster pulls it off! With what economy he plants the "Schlegel" name, chosen for symbolic reasons, in realistic earth! "Poor Emily (or die Engländerin)," for example, deftly indicates not only the respective attitudes but the vocal tones of the English and German relatives who had objected some 30 years earlier to the international marriage of Ernst Schlegel and Emily Pryce. How skillfully, too, he combines narrative and theme: like England, Germany also required

connections—between the Germany of the little courts that had nourished Bach, Goethe, Herder, Schiller, and Liszt, and the pan-Germanic
state that had annexed Alsace-Lorraine and was at that time intent on
commercial expansion and colonial conquest.

And yet, viewed as "text" rather than as "work," the long paragraph providing the Schlegel background is an imported fragment, a
minihistory of Germany in the nineteenth century, that Forster was
well competent to write, in part perhaps because of his own experience
in 1905 as a tutor to the children of the Countess von Arnim-Schlagenthin at the family estate in Nassenheide, Pomerania. The fragment
begins when the narrator (typically cavalier with respect to point of
view) rather abruptly states: "A word on their origin" (29). The end
of the fragment is more skillfully joined to the narrative; it is "dramatized" rather than "told," in a way that James would approve. Ernst
Schlegel's speech to the German nephew is heard by the young Margaret as she sits on the nephew's knee: ' "What's that? Your universities?
Oh yes, you have learned men, who collect more facts than do the
learned men of England. They collect facts, and facts, and empires of
facts. But which of them will rekindle the light within?' To all this
Margaret listened" (30). As, of course, does the reader, equally the
recipient of Ernst's wisdom on the evils of an exclusively empirical
education. Or is it Forster's wisdom? Perhaps it is Dickens's. The
German professors Ernst excoriates sound more than a little like
Thomas Gradgrind in *Hard Times* (1854), who opens Dickens's novel
with these words: "Now, what I want is, Facts. Teach these boys and
girls nothing but Facts. Facts alone are wanted in life. Plant nothing
else, and root out everything else. You can only form the minds of
reasoning animals upon Facts."[7] But no specific source need be invoked
for the attack on Benthamite empiricism that Forster puts into the
mouth of his idealistic German, just as no source need be posited for
Ernst-Forster's Arnoldian (or possibly Quaker) argument that reason,
utility, and science should be tempered by the light of the imagination.
The essayistic and intertextual dimensions of Ernst's speech are nevertheless present and, once recognized, qualify both the realism of the
scene and its claim to being a fully integrated part of the novel.

Since the analysis practiced above may seem to run against the grain of Forster's formalist fictional aims, I should give brief attention here to his aesthetic views (reserving a consideration of his attitude toward plot for the next chapter). It is true that in *Aspects of the Novel* (1927) and in some essays and lectures, such as "Anonymity: An Enquiry" (1925), "The *Raison d'Etre* of Criticism in the Arts" (1947), and "Art for Art's Sake" (1949), Forster often appears as a formalist and an Aristotelian. Nor is this surprising when we recall that he was a member—if a somewhat peripheral member—of the Bloomsbury Group. For certain critics he shares a general commitment to the theory of "significant form" advanced in Clive Bell's *Art* (1914) and in the writings of Roger Fry. Wilfred Stone goes so far as to propose that Forster, in *Aspects*, was "trying to do for the novel what Fry tried to do for the plastic arts," and if this claim now seems implausible, Forster provided texts that give it a measure of credibility.[8] "A work of art," he wrote in 1949, "whatever else it may be—is a self-contained entity, with a life of its own imposed on it by its creator. It has internal order."[9]

Forster seldom wrote about the novel, however, with the formalist enthusiasm that he did when he spoke more generally of Art. It may be that while reading the *Ancient Mariner* we enter "a universe that only answers to its own laws, supports itself, internally coheres, and has a new standard of truth." But the *Ancient Mariner* is a poem existing at the "atmosphere" end of the spectrum; the novel is nearer the other end, labeled "information," which includes "works of learning, history, sociology, philosophy, psychology, science, etc." and beyond these, newspapers, advertisements, and notices. Whatever else it may be, the novel is "partly a notice board."[10] As a figure for the novel, "notice board" has suggestive implications to readers conversant with Bakhtin's idea of the novel as a hybrid genre characterized by heteroglossia (many voices) and dialogism (the exchange of viewpoints); a notice board, it need hardly be elaborated, is not a figure for a formally integrated work of art; it is not a well-wrought urn.

If the novel is partly a notice board, then we may expect to uncover in its form a good deal of unintegrated information. Forster's goal, as the author of a "work," was to assimilate and dramatize such information, make it the stuff of his characters' thoughts and actions, and so arrange it that it contributed to the advancement of his narrative. But he did not always achieve this goal; as the *Nation*'s reviewer noted in 1910, his "dove-tailing" was sometimes too obvious. Nor, I believe, did he intend a complete—Jamesian—assimilation of his materials.

In a recent interesting article, Paul Rivenberg notes that *Howards End* is filled with essays and commentaries that often treat the same topics (places, literature, music) treated in Forster's essays. Rivenberg is scandalized by his own proposition, however, and contains it within a formalist notion of the novel as an organic structure. Worried by the idea that the novel's essays may merely be "the undisciplined ramblings of an author, who, having written essays since 1900, cannot help but riddle his novel with authorial comment," Rivenberg seeks and finds a principle of unity. As Margaret within the novel seeks to connect with other characters, so Forster as the author seeks to connect with the reader; though Forster may not achieve a Jamesian illusion of reality, he is "not out to destroy the illusion, just to pierce it."[11]

I agree with Rivenberg that Forster often successfully disguised his essays and commentaries by attaching them to the speeches or thoughts of his characters. But whether he achieved an overall unity of effect and consistency of voice may be doubted. As Rivenberg notes, Forster did pierce the illusion of his novel's reality. His narrator, as I shall show in chapter 9, often signals to the reader the constructed character of the novel. But even when the narrator does not invite a decomposition of the work—when he stitches the seams finely or carefully dovetails the joints—we may find interest in the novel's heterogeneous character.

In subsequent chapters, I shall consider more obvious instances of the novel's discursive heterogeneity, but here it is useful to analyze a scene that is often read as a synecdochic representation of Forster's belief—expressed in "The Challenge of Our Time"—that art is valuable because "it has to do with order, and creates little worlds of its own, possessing internal harmony, in the bosom of this disordered planet."[12] The scene—perhaps the most famous set piece in Forster's oeuvre—takes place at the Queen's Hall during a performance of Beethoven's Fifth Symphony. In describing the form and effects of Beethoven's symphony, Forster—or so critics have argued—is describing the form and effects of his novel. The scene is well integrated into the novel's plot, characterization, and themes, but the narrator's presence is also announced (almost as a wink to the reader) in the description of the Queen's Hall as the "dreariest music-room in London, though not as dreary as the Free Trade Hall, Manchester" (32).

In a way he may have learned from Jane Austen,[13] Forster evaluates the characters by discriminating among their responses to the concert: the philistine Mrs. Munt taps her feet "surreptitiously" to the music; the imaginative and emotional Helen sees "heroes and shipwrecks in the music's flood"; the cerebral Tibby holds the full score open on his knee; Fräulein Mosebach, the German cousin, remembers that Beethoven is "echt Deutsch"; her fiancé "can remember nothing but Fräulein Mosebach"; only Margaret responds to the music as music (32).

What we have is a spectrum of responses, more or less aesthetic, to a "significant" musical form, and the episode's textual character is suggested by its dialogical function in a Bloomsbury context. Of the three Schlegel responses, Helen's romantic response is most suspect in a Bloomsbury view. Tibby's, on the other hand, is excessively intellectual even for a Bloomsbury figure like Fry, whose aesthetic sensibility was, in Clive Bell's retrospective opinion, too scientific and methodical.[14] Margaret, "who can only see the music as music" (32), might seem to be the Bloomsbury norm, but Forster does not develop her response theoretically in chapter 5. It may be that Bell did, four years after *Howards End*, in his *Art*: "I am sure that the profounder subtleties of harmony and rhythm more often than not escape me [no Tibby he]. . . . But at moments I do appreciate music as pure musical form, as sounds combined according to the laws of a mysterious necessity, as pure art with a tremendous significance of its own and no relation whatever to the significance of life [no Helen he]."[15]

Yet we may well doubt that this Bloomsbury position is Forster's position. In his 1939 essay "Not Listening to Music," Forster reveals himself to have Helen's as well as Margaret's blood in his veins: even as he states that "the music which is untrammelled and untainted by reference is obviously the best sort of music to listen to," he admits that Beethoven's Seventh Symphony invokes for him "a grey-green tapestry of hunting scenes." "Only a purist," he adds, "would condemn all visual parallels, all emotional labellings, all programmes." Moreover, recalling his tendency to think "How like Monet!" when listening to Debussy, and "How like Debussy!" when looking at Monet, he plays a role in the essay exactly similar to Helen's in the novel.[16] As Margaret complains to Leonard Bast on their walk to Wickham Place from the Queen's Hall: "Helen's one aim is to translate tunes into the language of painting, and pictures into the language of music. It's very ingenious ... but what's gained, I'd like to know? ... If Monet's really Debussy, and Debussy's really Monet, neither gentleman is worth his salt—that's my opinion" (40).

Partly because he is not a Bloomsbury purist about musical form, Forster chooses Helen to "interpret" Beethoven's Fifth through her words and reported thoughts; but Helen's dramatic visualizations also have greater narrative appeal. After the Andante has come to an end, Tibby implores his companions in the Queen's Hall to "look out for the transitional passage on the drum," but Helen replies: "No; look out for the part where you think you have done with the goblins and they come back" (33–34). Her comment initiates the four paragraphs that compose the interpretation of the symphony.

The paragraphs are written in the *style indirect libre*, the flexible third-person discourse that allows an author to be mimetic and diegetic at once, that is, to imitate the pattern and texture of a character's thoughts while retaining the prerogative of distancing himself from those thoughts. In *Howards End*, the *style indirect libre* is also Forster's chief means of stitching information into his narrative fabric.

In the first paragraph, we are firmly in Helen's consciousness: not only is her name repeated, but "panic and emptiness!"—first used in describing Paul Wilcox and the Wilcox family at breakfast following Helen's short-lived engagement to Paul—is her phrase: "[The goblins] were not aggressive creatures; it was that that made them so terrible to Helen. They merely observed in passing that there was no such thing as splendour or heroism in the world. . . . Helen could not contradict them, for once . . . she had . . . seen the reliable walls of youth collapse. Panic and emptiness! Panic and emptiness!" (34).

In the second paragraph, the *style indirect libre* remains centered in Helen's consciousness as the language, refusing a main verb in one sentence, seeks to emulate in words the magnificence of Beethoven's music.

> For, as if things were going too far, Beethoven took hold of the goblins and made them do what he wanted. He appeared in person. He gave them a little push, and they began to walk in a major key instead of in a minor, and then—he blew with his mouth and they were scattered! Gusts of splendour, gods and demigods contending with vast swords, colour and fragrance broadcast on the field of battle, magnificent victory, magnificent death! Oh, it all burst before the girl, and she even stretched out her gloved hands as if it was tangible. (34)

In the third paragraph, though Helen is not named, "panic and emptiness!" is, and like a leitmotiv in Wagner that recalls the ring or the sword, the phrase implies Helen's continuing presence and consciousness. And yet, the reader may be beginning to wonder whether the interpretation is not Forster's as well. The distance between character and narrator—between mimesis and diegesis—has closed, as the use of the impersonal pronoun *one* suggests; Forster could easily have written "Helen heard," not "one heard." "And the goblins—they had not really been there at all? . . . Beethoven knew better. The goblins really had been there. . . . It was as if the splendour of life might boil over and waste to steam and froth. In its dissolution one heard the terrible, ominous note, and a goblin, with increased malignity, walked quietly over the universe from end to end. Panic and emptiness! Panic and emptiness!" (34–35).

In the fourth paragraph, neither "Helen" nor her leitmotiv appears, and the use of the impersonal pronoun and the present tense in the last sentence ("that is why one can trust Beethoven") seems to lift the commentary from its mimetic context in Helen's consciousness to the status of a diegetic generalization carrying Forster's imprimatur. (Simply replacing Forster's words with "that was why Helen could trust Beethoven" restores the mimetic context.) "Beethoven chose to make all right in the end. . . . He brought back the gusts of splendour, the heroism, the youth, the magnificence of life and death, and, amid vast roarings of a superhuman joy, he led his Fifth Symphony to its conclusion. But the goblins were there. They could return. He had said so bravely, and that is why one can trust Beethoven when he says other things" (35).

Two points may be developed from the above analysis. The first is that Forster, a fine amateur pianist and musicologist, incorporated into his novel a brilliant impressionistic essay on Beethoven's Fifth Symphony.[17] Second, he did this very well, finding, in Russian formalist terms, a "motivation" for the essay in the character, attitudes, and thought rhythms of Helen Schlegel. The shifts to the impersonal pronoun and the present tense are not loudly announced. He did not have a composition ready to hand—as Sterne did, for example, when he used for Yorick's sermon in *Tristram Shandy* the actual sermon he had preached in York Minster at the close of the summer assizes in 1750. Forster's essay ("Not Listening to Music") appeared thirty years after the novel; and yet the important recognition is that an essayistic discourse is perceptible in chapter 5, stitched skillfully into the story through the *style indirect libre*.[18] Not only is Helen an appropriate vessel of consciousness for the pictorial interpretation of the symphony, but the concert is the occasion of "goblin footfalls" entering the lives of the Schlegel sisters: it is at the Queen's Hall that they encounter Leonard Bast, the impecunious clerk and aspirant to culture who lives just above the "abyss" of poverty, and who as an indirect result of this meeting will come to a tragic end.

So successful is the stitching of the essay discourse into the narrative in chapter 5 that some readers have found the symphony to be an expression of Forster's faith in the ordering powers of fiction: as Beethoven in the Fifth Symphony both expresses and, through musical form, contains the "goblins" (a figure for the nihilism that stalks human ideals of beauty and worth), so Forster in *Howards End* both expresses and, through fictional form, contains the "panic and emptiness" (a catchphrase signifying his Conradian apprehension of the horrors that exist behind the facade of an imperialist civilization). To respond in this way, however, may be to misread the claims for art made in chapter 5; just after the four paragraphs interpreting the symphony, Forster continues: "The music summed up to [Helen] all that had happened or could happen in her career. She read it as a tangible statement, which could never be superseded. The notes meant this and that to her, and they could have no other meaning, and life could have no other meaning" (35). Here Forster forsakes the mimetic and sympathetic functions of the *style indirect libre* and uses it to underscore instead the absolutist tendencies in Helen's personality (as the words *all*, *never*, and *no other* emphasize). To art and life both she responds with a determinate sense of what is right and true; this attitude will lead her to extreme opinions and actions in the novel. After an initial attraction, she will refuse *all* connection with the Wilcoxes. Placing *all* the blame for Leonard Bast's ruin on Mr. Wilcox, she will drag Leonard and his wife to Evie Wilcox's wedding reception in faraway Shropshire in a quite unsuccessful attempt to shock Mr. Wilcox into acquiring a social conscience.

We can also look at the last cited paragraph as a comment on the dangers of determinate reading. No more than life is art subject to single constructions; a novel is not, any more than a symphony, a "tangible statement" meaning *this and that* and possessing *no other meaning*. Its powers to harmonize moral, social, and metaphysical problems (to contain the goblins) are limited, though still worth affirming. In this view, the symphony retains its synecdochic role, but the whole of which it is the significant part is not the unified aesthetic form producing (or trying and failing to produce) a coherent humanistic message.

In keeping with this recognition, I hold out no expectation that *Howards End* is a formal whole that proceeds by probable and necessary connections toward a single moral, social, or political position.

In the chapters that follow, however, as I treat separately various aspects of the novel (plot, setting, characterization, conversation, the narrator), while also attending to the recurring themes of money, sex, and culture, I assume that *Howards End* is of more interest to us today as a text than as a work. I begin with plot—that aspect of the novel that has proved contentious from the beginning. Plot is not the soul of *Howards End* (as Aristotle considered plot to be the soul of tragedy) because it does not prove to be, in the end, an informing principle of unity and connection. Rather than being a matter of regret, however, the refusal of *Howards End*'s plot to meet conventional expectations may become a focus of critical attention. Instead of assuming that *Howards End* is an organic whole, we may appreciate it as an assemblage of parts. Instead of revering the novel as a well-wrought urn (that is, until we discover flaws in its surface), we may respect it as a notice board that provides a great deal of interesting material, not all of which is congruent or even acceptable to us as readers.

5

Plot

"The king died and then the queen died" is a story. "The king died, and then the queen died of grief" is a plot.

—*Aspects of the Novel* (86)

Forster's famous distinction between story (the primitive aspect of narrative that possesses the simple but not despicable merit of keeping the reader interested in what happens next) and plot (a more complex form in which the emphasis falls on causality) suggests his respect for plot. His description of the novel as a "spongy tract" and a "low atavistic form" is reminiscent of Henry James's description of certain nineteenth-century novels as "large loose baggy monsters."[1] Both as a novelist and as a theorist of the novel, Forster was in some respects a Jamesian. In all of his novels he tried to avoid shapelessness, and in one at least he was influenced by James: the plot of *Where Angels Fear to Tread* (1905) owes much to that of *The Ambassadors* (1903). In his equally famous distinction between "flat" and "round" characters, he argues for a Jamesian (and Aristotelian) interdependence of character and plot; and in describing the "plot-maker," he would seem to be describing his own role in *Howards End*: "The plot-maker expects us to remember, we expect him to leave no loose ends. Every action or word ought to count; it ought to be economical and spare; even when complicated it should be organic and free from dead matter."[2]

Forster was more ambivalent about plot (and more critical of

James and Aristotle) than these remarks suggest, but for the moment it will be useful to observe the plot of *Howards End* in action, noting how Forster seeks to integrate character and episode, action and scene, and how all along he "hammer[s] away . . . at cause and effect."[3] To observe the plot, however, we need first to summarize the story on which it is superimposed.

Like that of *Sense and Sensibility* (1811), the story of *Howards End* concerns two sisters, different in temperament but united in their affection for one another; they fall in love with different kinds of men, hold different views on love and on the duty of the individual to society, and end up, after a period in which one sister retreats from social involvement, happily situated and close together in the same rural place. A significant difference between the stories is that, in *Howards End*, only one sister marries.[4]

"What the story does," Forster proposes, "is to narrate the life in time," and one way to describe the story of the Schlegel sisters is to sketch its chronology.[5] *Howards End* covers a period of five years, beginning and ending in the month of June. Despite a few minor inconsistencies, Forster sustains a sense of time passing, holidays occurring, university terms beginning and ending, people growing older, dying, marrying, going about their daily affairs. Forster's time is secular, urban, middle-class, and domestic; though his narrator deplores (in chapter 10) the commercialization of Christmas, his novel has little to do with the liturgical year, and though the countryside is of major importance to his vision of England, and the novel begins and ends during haytime, he does not—as Hardy does in his novels, for example—give much attention to seasonal or agricultural rhythms.

The first phase of the novel (chapters 1–12) takes place from June to Christmas in the novel's first year, when Margaret Schlegel is 29 years old and Helen 21. The novel begins with the dramatic visit of Helen to Howards End, the visit that brings about her sudden engagement to, and equally sudden disengagement from, Paul Wilcox. Thereafter (or "and then," as Forster, in *Aspects*, describes the typical story's development), the novel settles in London, where the Schlegel sisters, their 16-year-old brother Tibby, their visiting aunt, and, for a while, their German cousins live the kind of cultured Edwardian existence that people with comfortable unearned incomes might be expected to live: concerts, luncheon parties, discussion evenings, and the like. Interrupting this life of cultured leisure are two encounters. The first occurs in chapter 5 at the Queen's Hall; Helen, inspired by Beethoven's music, leaves the concert carrying Leonard Bast's umbrella. Leonard, not quite 21, is a clerk with the Porphyrion Fire Insurance Company and is lower-middle-class in appearance, speech, and behavior. But he is interested in cultural matters, and the encounter leads the progressive and socially concerned Schlegel sisters to think of their social obligations. Leonard, however, after recovering his umbrella from the Schlegels' flat in Wickham Place, leaves their lives again to return to his squalid home and nagging companion, Jacky, in Camelia Road.

The second encounter occurs when the Wilcoxes take out a lease on a modern flat in London across from the Schlegels' home (chapter 7). Now develops the friendship between Margaret and Mrs. Wilcox, a dignified, rather tired woman of 50; the friendship is terminated before Margaret can visit Howards End by the unexpected death of the older woman. The novel's first phase ends with Mrs. Wilcox's funeral and the decision of the Wilcox family to suppress her dying bequest of Howards End to Margaret.

An interval of over two years separates the novel's first phase from its second (chapters 13–31), which occupies another period of six months, from Easter to October. The two encounters of the first phase are repeated. Leonard reenters the sisters' lives when Jacky, now Leonard's wife, comes looking for him at Wickham Place; Leonard has left on a nocturnal walk, and Jacky, discovering the card that Margaret had earlier given Leonard, suspects he is with her. Mr. Wilcox reappears when he chances to meet Margaret and Helen one evening on the Chelsea Embankment. A tea at Wickman Place accidentally brings together Leonard and the Wilcoxes, in the persons of Mr. Wilcox and his daughter Evie (complete with romping puppies), but the meeting is not a success. Leonard, insecure and blustering, resents the Schlegels' inquiries about his work and, disappointed in his wish to talk of books with the Schlegel women, once more vanishes, though Helen keeps in touch with him through correspondence.

Now ensues the courtship of Margaret by the "elderly" Henry

Wilcox (he is 53!), his proposal to her, and her acceptance. Helen is dismayed, for ever since the fiasco with Mr. Wilcox's son Paul, she has considered the Wilcoxes to be morally empty figures. She and Henry fall out over some casual remarks he makes about the advisability of Leonard's leaving the Porphyrion; later, when that advice turns out badly, she angrily drags Leonard and Jacky to Evie Wilcox's wedding in Oniton. Helen means to gain restitution for the Basts, but her action has the unintended consequence of revealing a lurid episode in Henry's past: Jacky, in a drunken haze, recognizes him as her lover of an earlier time in Cyprus. A breach opens between the sisters, and Helen leaves, forgetting to pay the Basts' hotel bill or to give them their return tickets to London. Helen travels to Oxford, where she tells Tibby (now in his final year) to arrange for a large portion of her fortune to be made over to the Basts. Leonard, however, will refuse her charity. Meanwhile, despite the exposure of Henry's infidelity to his first wife, Margaret decides to go ahead with the marriage. She and Henry honeymoon in Innsbruck, but Helen, who is in Europe now, avoids meeting them, and the breach between the sisters widens.

Another interval of six months precedes the novel's third phase (chapters 32–43). Now it is the spring of the following year. Aunt Juley's serious illness brings Helen back to England, but, inexplicably, she still avoids her family. Margaret, concerned that Helen might be ill, is persuaded by Henry, against her better judgment, to lure Helen to Howards End. There Helen is discovered to be pregnant; it emerges that in an act of sympathy she had slept with Leonard on the night of Evie's wedding in Oniton. (Astute readers will hardly have failed to pick up on Forster's clues about the pregnancy: in a conversation between Margaret and Dolly in chapter 32, for example, the fact that Helen has been absent for eight months is stated three times.)

Henry responds to Helen's pregnancy with a moral indignation that Margaret trenchantly declares to be pernicious in view of his own sexual history. Against her husband's prohibition, Margaret spends the night with Helen at Howards End.

The following morning, two figures converge on Howards End: Charles Wilcox, Henry's elder son, who has learned the name of

Plot

Helen's seducer from Tibby, and Leonard Bast, who, filled with remorse, has come to seek some kind of absolution from Margaret. Their
convergence becomes a confrontation when Charles seizes a sword,
beats Leonard with the flat, and Leonard dies. Charles is found guilty
of manslaughter and sentenced to a term in prison. Finding Henry
broken by the news, Margaret reverses her decision to leave him and
instead takes him down to Howards End to recruit.

An interval of 14 months intervenes before the final chapter,
which takes place in June during haytime and describes the happy
existence of the sisters at Howards End. Margaret is a wife but has no
children, nor any wish for them; Helen is a mother but has no husband,
nor any wish for one. Together with a tired Henry, Helen's son, and
a boy from the neighboring farm, however, Margaret and Helen face
the future with hope. Howards End, denied to Margaret by the suppression of the legacy, comes to her now as a gift from her husband;
on her death the house will go to her nephew.

Summarizing the story of the novel in this linear way allows
us to detect the superimposed patterns of synchronic and diachronic
opposition that constitute the novel's plot. The synchronic opposition
is that between the Wilcoxes, representing the outer life—the practical
business mentality of the liberal imperialists of the time—and the
Schlegels, representing the inner life—the culture of the educated bourgeoisie, who, while sympathetic to the progressive platform of Lloyd
George, live a largely private existence devoted to art, music, and
literature. This opposition of ideologies, elaborated in impressively
detailed ways in the novel's characterization and dialogues, exists
because of the plot, which repeatedly brings the Wilcox and Schlegel
families together, revealing how both families impinge for better or
for worse on the Basts, who represent the novel's underclass.

The diachronic opposition is that between the older gemeinschaft
world, of which Mrs. Wilcox (née Ruth Howard) and Miss Avery are
the novel's sole representatives, and the gesellschaft world of the present and foreseeable future.[6] Though Mrs. Wilcox dies early in the
novel, and Miss Avery is a secondary character, the rural world they
represent, with its immemorial customs and traditions, is symbolized

by Howards End and the wych-elm tree. The communal heritage implied by this setting stands against the individualistic and contractual relationships of an increasingly urban civilization. If, symbolically, Mrs. Wilcox represents the past in its spiritual aspects, and the other Wilcoxes and the Schlegels different secular possibilities in the present, Leonard Bast is both the past and the present: his ancestors once lived and worked in the country, but his own existence in Camelia Road testifies to his social and spiritual impoverishment. Leonard, as the representative of the emerging masses, is the problem of the present and the future; but if in the present neither the Wilcoxes (who feel no responsibility for his welfare) nor the Schlegels (who altruistically intervene but to regrettable effect) improve his lot in life, the future, in a sense, belongs to him, since his son will inherit Howards End.

It is one thing to detect the patterns of Forster's plot, another to evaluate their success in providing moral and political connections. From the beginning, as we have seen, readers found the contrived nature of the novel's plot problematic. Leonard's seduction of Helen (or vice versa) and the manner of Leonard's death were particular sticking places, and the ending—as the objections of Crews and Stone, already discussed in chapter 3, show—posed major difficulties. For the *Nation*'s reviewer in 1910, there was "too much ingenious dovetailing of incidents, too much of accidental happenings, too much twisting and stretching and straining of human material for *Howards End* to rank high as a work of art."[7] Granting some truth to these charges, we may remain impressed by the remarkable economy of Forster's plotting. That it is *plotting*, however, we are unlikely to forget, especially if we recall Forster's distrust of plots, including his own.

Less than two years after *Howards End* was published, for example, he wrote to Forest Reid: "As for 'story' I never yet did enjoy a novel or play in which someone didn't tell me afterward that there was something wrong with the story, so that's going to be no drawback as far as I'm concerned. 'Good Lord, why am I so bored?'—'I know; it must be the plot developing harmoniously.' So I often reply to myself, and there rises before me my special nightmare—that of the writer as craftsman, natty and deft."[8] Later, addressing the Bloomsbury Memoir Club, he declined to explain "the various tricks and processes—many of them disingenuous—by which Life is transmuted into a Forster Novel."[9]

What Forster chose to conceal—his "tricks and processes," and the "faking" he also speaks of in his memoir as necessary to the achievement of an even fictional surface—I now wish to begin analyzing and evaluating. (*Begin*; since plot relates to each of the other aspects of *Howards End* considered in this study, my analysis and evaluation of its effects will be ongoing.)

We may consider, first, the novel's rhythm, which is not—as the chronological summary suggests—regular and even but variable in tempo and intensity. Certain sequences, such as Helen's initial visit to and departure from Howards End (chapters 1 and 3), Evie's wedding (chapters 25–30), and the events leading up to Leonard's death (chapters 34–42), occupy brief but intensely experienced periods of time. Helen's stay at Howards End, for example, is from the Tuesday of one week to the Monday of the next. In these sequences, the action is swift, and both mimesis (in the form of letters, speech, and dialogue) and diegesis (the narration of personal encounters and decisive happenings) enliven the narration as they bring the novel to moments of climax.

Separable from these action-filled sequences are more leisurely and detachable chapters—dramatic in another sense—in which characters meet and talk and thereby reveal their characteristic strengths and weaknesses. In chapter 11, for example, the surviving Wilcoxes gather after the funeral of Mrs. Wilcox to deal ("item by item") with the "deceased's" will. It is not that action is wholly absent from these chapters, any more than that conversation is wholly absent from the action chapters. The suppression of Mrs. Wilcox's bequest of Howards End to Margaret is obviously crucial to the plot. Rather, action in these chapters is secondary to the dialogues occurring in domestic settings. Several of these chapters, in fact, center on a meal: the breakfast over which Margaret and Mrs. Munt discuss how to deal with the news of Helen's having fallen in love with Paul (chapter 2); the unsuccessful luncheon party that Margaret and Helen give in honor of Mrs. Wilcox (chapter 9); the even less successful tea that the sisters give for Leonard (chapter 16); the luncheon at Simpson's in the Strand at which Henry begins his courtship of Margaret (chapter 17); or that other luncheon in Tibby's Oxford lodgings during which Helen announces her plan to give away a large portion of her fortune to the Basts (chapter 30).

In such "tea-tabling" chapters Forster's powers of mimesis are extraordinarily impressive.[10] Chapter 15, for example, featuring the debate over dinner among the members of the informal discussion club, is not only a fine synecdochic treatment of a question at the heart of the novel—what economic system is most beneficial to the poor?—it is also a nuanced and critical representation of class speech, the "sociolect" of the progressive and educated bourgeoisie. As such, the chapter has little or nothing to do with the novel's plot, though a great deal to do with the novel's themes. Forster's mimesis—evident in the remarkable conversations of *Howards End*—deserves separate treatment, and I shall return to this aspect in chapter 8, though I shall shortly indicate here how diegesis and mimesis combine to excellent effect in a specific scene.

Also separable from those swiftly paced action sequences are numerous passages of commentary by the narrator, who appears in a great variety of roles in *Howards End*. He provides, for example, eulogies of the London railway stations (chapter 2); ekphrastic descriptions of Dorset (chapter 19) and Hertfordshire (chapter 23) ("ekphrasis" being the term used by the student of rhetoric for structured praise of the scenery); and sage assessments of a whole gamut of political or social issues. At such times, chronology is suspended and the action stopped as the narrator speaks not in one voice but in several and his audience is not a homogeneous readership but a series of posited or anticipated readers whose various views are dialogically engaged. This heterogeneous narrative commentary is distinct from (and may be at odds with) the mimesis of conversations, but like the conversations, it is a recursive rather than linear feature of the narrative; its relation to plot may be cooperative, or disjunctive, or redundant. Like the novel's conversations, the narrative commentary deserves separate treatment; see chapter 9.

Having bracketed off conversations and narrative commentary, we return to the action sequences, recognizing that Forster often quickens the tempo of his plot so as to conceal his didactic intentions. It is, for example, very improbable that Henry Wilcox should participate in the ruin not only of Leonard Bast but, separately and earlier, of Leonard's wife. Forster's intention is to expose several kinds of exploitation perpetrated by British imperialists like Henry: the exploitation of the poor at home by managerial capitalism; the exploitation of lower-class women by upper-class men; and the exploitation of other nations (Henry's sexual adventure takes place in Cyprus) by colonial entrepreneurs. Helen may be misguided in dragging the Basts to Oniton; indeed, her progressive sympathies are undercut when she leaves the Basts without paying for their hotel or giving them their return train tickets. But the confrontation she stages is necessary to Forster's critique of Wilcoxite capitalism, as the following climax shows:

> Henry went up to the woman. She raised her face, which gleamed in the twilight like a puff-ball.
> "Madam, you will be more comfortable at the hotel," he said sharply.
> Jacky replied: "If it isn't Hen!"
> "Ne crois pas que le mari lui ressemble," apologized Margaret. "Il est tout à fait différent."
> "Henry!" she repeated, quite distinctly. . . .
> "Why does she call you 'Hen'?" said Margaret innocently. "Has she ever seen you before?"
> "Seen Hen before!" said Jacky. "Who hasn't seen Hen? He's serving you like me, my dear. These boys! You wait—still we love 'em." (242–43)

In this scene, what might have been merely an allegory of the oppression of one class and sex by another is humanized and complicated. Margaret's delayed awareness of the situation—a function of her sexual and social innocence—is well conveyed, and in other ways the scene is a manifest improvement on the very melodramatic and sketchy manuscript draft. New in the novel, for example, are Margaret's remarks in French: not only do these characterize Margaret and her class as against the cockney speech of Jacky, but they are an incrimination of Margaret, who at this point in the novel is repelled by Jacky even as she wishes to recommend the more deserving Leonard to her husband's notice. True, Margaret's French is idiomatic, unlike Henry's *pas devant les domestiques* French on the occasion of Helen's occupation of Howards End ("Il faut dormir sur ce sujet" [310]), and the fact testifies once more to her intellectual superiority to her husband. But her correct French hardly excuses her from the charge of exacerbating the very social differences she elsewhere wishes to erase. The Oniton episode, in other words, calls into question the possibility of connections between progressive, as well as imperialistic liberals and the urban poor. Moreover, with remarkable narrative economy, it also subdivides progressive liberalism into radical (Helen) and moderate (Margaret) wings and the urban poor into deserving (Leonard) and undeserving (Jacky) branches; all of which dramatizes the difficulties facing any goal of social harmony. For it is not only predatory capitalists like Henry who retard the advancement of the underclass but well-meaning humanitarians like Helen and Margaret. Culture, as well as capitalism, can exclude the poor. The Oniton episode raises the ominous possibility that culture may not be a critical Arnoldian force calling modern civilization to an awareness of its moral and political responsibility to a whole society; despite its best intentions, culture may be complicitous with the social Darwinist attitudes typical of laissez-faire capitalism. Margaret is repeatedly aware that culture depends upon money; but she is not aware, on this occasion, that culture, like money, is a currency—a medium of exchange favoring the survival of those who possess a command of language over those who lack linguistic skills. (For Margaret's awareness elsewhere that culture is in danger of becoming *merely* a medium of exchange, see her speech to Henry at Simpson's in the Strand—discussed in chapter 8.)

Even more "plotted" than the encounter of Henry and Jacky at Oniton, however, is Leonard's death in chapter 41. This scene, the dramatic climax of the novel, evidently caused Forster difficulties. Working notes in the manuscripts reveal that even after writing six chapters Forster was uncertain about exactly who was to die at Howards End:

> Then I think that Charles [goes] is sent by his father to horse whip Leonard, and is killed by him, and L flings himself out of the window.
> Or it may be that Helen & Leonard die.
> Or perhaps Leonard lives.[11]

Having decided on Leonard as victim, Forster still faced the task of concealing his climax's diagrammatic nature. Leonard dies when Charles beats him with the sword that had once belonged to Ernst Schlegel and when, at the same time, the Schlegel books fall on top of him. Though Charles is convicted of manslaughter, neither his action nor the falling books would have killed Leonard had the latter not been constitutionally incapable of withstanding these assaults. In Leonard's triply caused death, Forster indicts the seizure and misuse of power by imperialists, the hostility of culture to the lower classes, and an uncaring society in which the urban poor are physically as well as economically and culturally vulnerable. It is a very allegorical climax; and allegory being out of place in realistic fiction, Forster has to speed up his narrative tempo in order to carry his readers with him.

He faced an earlier problem, however: how to bring together, in the same place and at the same time, the major participants of the drama, all of whom are, thematically speaking, factors in Leonard's death. It would be tedious to recall in detail all the "tricks and processes" by which Forster brings to Howards End the widely dispersed characters of Helen, Margaret, Charles, and Leonard himself (Miss Avery is already there). A few observations, however, will suggest the complexity of the plotting. Leonard, having lost touch with the Schlegels, has to track Margaret down, and his difficulties allow Forster to show the social and geographical distances separating the classes in the Edwardian period. Charles, projecting his anger against the Schlegel sisters onto the seducer of Helen, has to discover the latter's identity. That their respective searches should eventuate in a simultane-

ous arrival at Howards End is, of course, improbable. But even more
unlikely is Helen's presence there. Determined at all costs to conceal
the scandal of her pregnancy, and relieved to learn that Aunt Juley's
illness is not terminal, Helen intends to return to Europe. Why then
does she not? Because she wishes to take one or two of her books
with her, and these (for other improbable reasons) are now stored at
Howards End. But why, since Mrs. Wilcox is dead and Henry and
Charles Wilcox have little love for the house, is Howards End still in
the family's possession?

The blunt answer is that Forster needs it to be. Indeed, if the plot
can be said to serve any single "end," it is Howards End. Here the story
begins and ends, attempts at connection are made, various epiphanies
occur, and the violent climax takes place. Even when the action is
elsewhere—in London, or Dorset, or Shropshire—Howards End remains in reserve for the author as a privileged place, the necessary site,
evidently, of a difficult transition from gemeinschaft to gesellschaft,
the necessary ground on which intellectuals and imperialists meet,
collide, move apart, and come together in the end, to the extent, and
in the only ways, that a reconciliation is possible.

Howards Ends as metonym—as a complex "container" for Forster's values—is the subject of the next chapter. Here I describe how
Forster keeps the house at the center of the novel's business—by means
of Hamar Bryce, a character who, to my knowledge, has received no
attention from the critics, and with good reason. He never speaks, and
he is never seen. Not only is he not a round character, he is not even
flat. Who is he? He is the tenant of Howards End through the middle
part of the novel, after the house is vacated by the Wilcoxes following
Mrs. Wilcox's death and funeral in chapter 11, and before it becomes,
from chapter 33 onward, the scene of a series of events, culminating
in the death of Leonard Bast. Hamar Bryce becomes the butt of Mr.
Wilcox's anger when he presumes to sublet the house without permission, and when he puts up "To Let" notices he precipitates a display
of violence by Charles Wilcox, who flings the boards down.

Less a character than a device to evoke responses from the "real"
characters in the novel, he is even more important to the progress of

Forster's plot. Here his role is to keep the house empty and available for whatever events—and meanings—Forster chooses to stage there. Because Hamar Bryce has rented it, Howards End is not occupied by a Wilcox, even though it would be natural for Charles, with a wife and a growing family, to move in after his mother's death. It would also be prudent, given their suppression of Mrs. Wilcox's legacy of the house to Margaret. In order *not* to have Charles, or another Wilcox, move into Howards End, Forster has therefore to do some explaining: the Wilcoxes are nomadic, they collect houses, they do not settle; besides, Howards End lacks modern conveniences. Since Paul has a feeling for the place, however, Mr. Wilcox lets rather than sells it. But he lets it to an invalid who has been ordered abroad for his health and is ready to die whenever Forster decides the plot requires it. This occurs in chapter 31, at the time of Margaret's marriage to Mr. Wilcox and the Schlegels' forced removal from Wickham Place. We learn that "Mr. Bryce had died abroad—an unsatisfactory affair," and that until the house is relet, "the Schlegels [are] welcome to stack their furniture in the garage and lower rooms" (269).

And so, thanks to Hamar Bryce's timely demise, and however improbably, the Schlegel furniture and books come to Howards End, to be set out there by Miss Avery, to trick Helen to come to the house in her pregnancy, to furnish the stage for Margaret's defense of Helen against her husband and the setting for the sisters' night together, and to participate in the death of Leonard Bast. "No wonder," as Forster might say, "that nothing is heard but hammering and screwing."[12] Without Hamar Bryce the novel would lack its crisis, crescendo, and climax.

Yet, sheer device that he is, Hamar Bryce receives from Forster the attention of a realist. The name, first, is a perfect Jamesian name, irreducibly realistic, resisting all allegorical translations.[13] In addition, "Hamar Bryce" becomes human in inverse proportion to his dehumanization at the hands of the Wilcoxes, who treat him in strictly contractual ways. "What's Mr. Bryce like?" Margaret asks. But neither Henry nor Charles replies. "Mr. Bryce was the tenant, who had no right to sublet; to have defined him further was a waste of time" (206). One can only admire the bravura of a novelist who, having created a narrative function, criticizes those who treat that function in functional ways. By such means "work" strives to wrest a measure of aesthetic autonomy from "text."

Hamar Bryce's function is to keep Howards End available for its true inheritor, Margaret. Unlike the Wilcoxes, who "have all decided against Howards End," Margaret (like Fanny Price in *Mansfield Park* [1814]) respects the values of a heritage that is not her own. "When you moved out of Howards End," she tells Henry, "I should have moved Mr. Charles Wilcox into it. I should have kept so remarkable a place in the family" (142). In the end, it is she, not Charles, who moves into Howards End, along with Henry (her much diminished husband), Helen, and Helen's child by Leonard Bast—the child who will inherit the house.

What the ending means depends in significant part on the meaning—or meanings—of the setting in which it takes place, as well as on the characters who finally inhabit it. In the next chapter I shall consider the novel's setting, and in the chapter following the characters. But before concluding this discussion of the plot I should raise the question of whether we need to interpret novel's ending as Forster's final word, his ultimate connection. If we seek to accord it this privilege, the ending is likely to disappoint: unlike "average" endings, of which Forster speaks in *Aspects of the Novel*,[14] it does not close with a death or a marriage, and the idyllic final scene is qualified by the "red rust" of suburbia, which appears beyond the meadow (355). Moreover, in terms of conviction, the final chapter yields in intensity to an earlier chapter.

The renewed relationship between the sisters at Howards End, in chapter 37, is the deepest and most convincing of all the connections made in the novel, though I recognize that, like the ending it adumbrates, it provides us with a circumscribed and domestic vision, an enclave of happiness protected from society at large. For critics who want Forster to achieve more ambitious social connections with the masculine world of business and commerce, the peace and happiness between the sisters will seem incomplete. For those who recognize the force of his critique of patriarchal obtuseness and insensitivity, however, the haven in which the sisters find a temporary calm may constitute a severe indictment of a brutal world that ostracizes unmarried mothers while condoning male promiscuity. This indeed is the burden of Margaret's criticism of her husband when he seeks to prevent Helen from staying the night (322). Forster's affirmation in chapter 37 may be domestic and female in character; but it is assuredly not fainthearted, as I shall discuss further in chapter 7 when I consider Forster's critique of heterosexual monogamy as a fictional and social norm. Now it is time to turn to the setting that gives the novel its title.

Rooksnest and the wych-elm tree

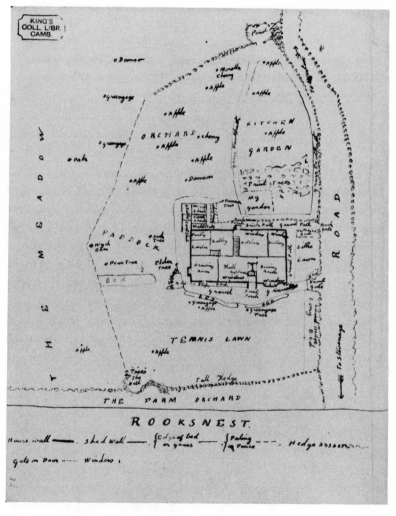

Forster's map of the Rooksnest garden

6

Setting

It certainly was a lovable little house, and still is, though it now
stands just outside a twentieth-century hub and almost within sound
of a twentieth-century hum.

—*Marianne Thornton* (269)

Like Jane Austen's *Mansfield Park, Howards End* takes its title from
the name of a country house, and like many other English novels, from
Samuel Richardson's *Sir Charles Grandison* (1754) to Evelyn Waugh's
Brideshead Revisited (1945) and beyond, it uses a house not only as
the background of action and characterization but as a metonym for an
approved form of society. Grandison Hall, Brambleton Hall, Waverley
Honour, Tully Veolan, Wuthering Heights, Thrushcross Grange,
Thornfield, Ullathorne Court, Grandcourt, Poynton, Medley, Bladesover, Groby, Crome: the list could be tripled without exhausting our
sense of the significant roles houses have played in the history of
English fiction.

As metonyms, such houses may promote a variety of political
programs, including progressive ones. George Eliot, for example, in
Felix Holt (1866), makes Transome Hall serve liberal ends, and William Morris, in *News from Nowhere* (1890), transforms country
houses into collegial dwellings in the interests of a socialist vision. But
the fictional country house more usually serves conservative purposes,
as in the novels of Jane Austen, Walter Scott, and Henry James; though
these purposes may differ from author to author and from period to

period, they usually entail—as *Howards End* entails—the identification of political threats to a traditional moral order that the fictional house, in a more or less healthy way, embodies.[1]

In the "intertext" of fictional houses, Howards End takes on its distinctive—and often conservative—meanings; such houses are the tradition in relation to which Forster's individual talent found expression. Like Scott, for example, he uses place as a forum where the opposition between traditional ideals and an increasingly urban and commercial civilization can be debated and, if possible, reconciled. And like Austen, he uses garden and house improvements as a way of criticizing the destructive effects of free-market capitalism on a traditional society based in a rural community. This is not to say that Forster's choice of setting made it impossible for his novel to accommodate liberal ideals; it is to say that the focus on an old house and a wych-elm tree gives to *Howards End* a conservative cast that is antipathetic to technological progress and the rapacious economic individualism characteristic of modern society.

Shortly, I shall analyze Howards End as symbolic representation, but first I should recall that the house is, in remarkable ways, a reconstruction of Forster's childhood home. Howards End is based on Rooksnest, an old red-brick farmhouse near Stevenage in Hertfordshire. As the photograph at the head of this chapter shows, Rooksnest was (and is) a modest house—very different from the baroque Castle Howard, which is partly the model for Brideshead in *Brideshead Revisited*, or Audley End, the great Jacobean mansion, not far from Stevenage, which shares with Howards End nothing but the designation of "end."

Forster lived in Rooksnest with his mother from age four to age fourteen. Shortly after his unwilling departure in 1893, Forster wrote a memoir about the house and sketched a map of the house, lawn, garden, and meadow.[2] The map shows the location of the paddock and the wych-elm tree, as well as of pear trees, apple trees, and greengage trees. The memoir includes other details that the novel, beginning with Helen's letters in the first chapter, repeats: for example, the fine view to the west, the vine that covers the house, and inside, the door that opens from the hall to the hidden staircase that rises like a tunnel to the first floor. In the memoir, as in Helen's letter, there are three bedrooms on the first floor, with three attics above; the middle bedroom of the first floor—the same bedroom in which Helen's child is born—corresponds to Forster's own childhood nursery. True, Helen in her early letter writes of nine windows, whereas photographs of Rooksnest show only eight; but the very fact that one notes the discrepancy testifies to the accuracy of Forster's transcription.

When Margaret first visits Howards End, she conducts, as it were, an inventory of its features: "There were the greengage trees . . . there the tennis lawn, there the hedge that would be glorious with dog-roses in June. . . . Down by the dell-hole . . . Lent lilies stood sentinel on its margin. . . . Tulips were a tray of jewels. She could not see the wych-elm tree, but a branch of the celebrated vine, studded with velvet knobs, had covered the porch" (208). When Margaret enters the house, she enters the space of Forster's childhood and enduring memory: "Drawing-room, dining-room and hall—how petty the names sounded! Here were simply three rooms where children could play and friends shelter from the rain" (209–10).

Of all fictional houses, Howards End seems closest to its model; H. G. Wells's Bladesover in *Tono Bungay*, based on the much grander Uppark where his mother was housekeeper, pales in comparison. At Howards End and Rooksnest, the farm is close to the house, the meadow is used for hay, animals stray onto the lawn, and even details that would seem surely to be inventions—such as the pig's teeth in the wych-elm tree—have their basis in Forster's experience, as the following comments, written when Forster was about 15, show:

> The most interesting thing in the garden was the wych-elm tree. It was of great height and had a very thick stem. . . . About four feet from the ground were three or four fangs stuck deep into the rugged bark. As far as I can make out these were votive offerings of people who had their toothache cured by chewing pieces of the bark, but whether they were their own teeth I don't know and certainly it does not seem likely that they should sacrifice one sound tooth as the price of having one aching one cured.[3]

In remarkable ways, then, Howards End is a real house, and the novel to which it gives its name testifies to the enduring moral power that an early environment can provide. *Howards End*, like the memoir and map of Rooksnest that preceded it, resembles the "surveyor's map of . . . lost fields and meadows" that Gaston Bachelard invites all of us to make; indeed, Bachelard's "topoanalysis" of house images is of great relevance to an understanding of Forster's novel and of the significance of Mrs. Wilcox. With the house image, Bachelard argues, "we are in possession of a veritable principle of psychological intergration." Forster would surely agree, as would Mrs. Wilcox (though her language would be simpler). When she learns that Margaret's home in Wickham Place is to be razed and replaced by luxury flats, she responds vehemently: "It is monstrous, Miss Schlegel; it isn't right. I had no idea that this was hanging over you. I do pity you from the bottom of my heart. To be parted from your house, your father's house—it oughtn't to be allowed. It is worse than dying" (86). What she deplores, in Bachelardian terms, is the loss of those "anthropocosmic" ties that find their first attachment in the "universe of the house."[4] What she represents in the novel ("you and I and Henry are only fragments of that woman's mind," says Margaret to Helen [328]) seems close to Bachelard's proposals concerning the values of the house: "In the life of a man, the house thrusts aside contingencies, its councils of continuity are unceasing. Without it, man would be a dispersed being. It maintains him through the storms of the heavens and through those of life. It is body and soul. It is the human being's first world. Before he is 'cast into the world' . . . man is laid in the cradle of the house."[5]

Forster was himself, on two occasions, "cast into the world" from the cradle of a house. Rooksnest in 1893 was the first. His departure from this beloved home was partly the consequence of the need to find for him a public school where he could be a day boy; Tonbridge in Kent fitted the need. At the same time, however, the landlord of Rooksnest seems to have declined to renew Mrs. Forster's lease on the house, and the departure was not amicable. West Hackhurst in 1945 was the second occasion, and though his removal from this house occurred long after he wrote *Howards End*, the loss of West Hackhurst is worthy of brief mention here. When his landlord declined to renew his lease, Forster was, in a real sense, parted from his "father's house," for West Hackhurst had been designed for his Aunt Laura by Forster's father; Aunt Laura bequeathed the lease to Forster on her death in 1924. After he left the house in 1945, he wrote another memoir in which, after describing a meeting of landowners intent on obstructing rural developments, he adds: "That was my nearest approach to feudalism. My next nearest had been at the age of fourteen, in the Howards End house in Hertfordshire. We were turned out of it. If the land had welcomed me then, if it had welcomed me more effectively at West Hackhurst, the Tory side of my character would have developed, and my liberalisms been atrophied."[6] Here a house is not so much the site of anthropocosmic connection as of "Tory" power. In 1945–46, during the social revolution conducted by the Labour party, Forster was aware that "the challenge of our time" involved difficult decisions about housing. A decade later, in another reminiscence of Rooksnest, he wrote: "The impressions received there . . . still glow . . . and have given me a slant upon society and history. It is a middle-class slant, atavistic . . . and it has been corrected by contact with friends who have never had a home in the Thornton sense, and do not want one."[7]

Forster's remarks should warn us not to approach his fictional house as if it were the transcendental site of spiritual values, presided over by Mrs. Wilcox as the tutelary deity. Forster invests Howards End with many qualities, and in the end we may wish to affirm the house's role as the locus of admirable social and even spiritual meanings. But on the way to that affirmation, we need to recognize—as Forster himself came to recognize more clearly—that Howards End represents, at base, a piece of real property. Furthermore, close as it is to its model, Rooksnest, Howards End is not a house composed of bricks and mortar; it is a structure of words—an occasion for ekphrasis (descriptive praise). As such, it exists in and takes meaning from a long tradition of politically charged fictional descriptions.

From the first sentence of Helen's letter in chapter 1 we learn that Howards End is not what Helen and Margaret had expected; the house is not "all gables and wiggles," and its garden is not "all gamboge-coloured paths" (3). Why had the Schlegel sisters expected these features? One answer is that Forster is working in a fictional tradition in which false taste in styles of house and garden is the mark of the nouveaux riches, whose city attitudes threaten traditional country ways. Howards End is not yet transformed by fashionable improvements because it belongs to Mrs. Wilcox—born a Howard—not to the plutocratic Wilcox men. After his mother's funeral, Charles thinks fondly of her: "How she had disliked improvements. . . . With what difficulty had they persuaded her to yield to them the paddock for [the garage]—the paddock that she[8] loved more dearly than the garden itself. The vine—she had got her way about the vine. It still encumbered the south wall with its unproductive branches" (96–97).

Because of Mrs. Wilcox, Howards End still appears to Helen as "old and little, and altogether delightful—red brick" (3). The house, still "encumbered" with a vine, is protected by a wych-elm tree. The tree stands on the boundary between garden and meadow, and nearby, a hedge of sweet-smelling dog-roses is straggly enough to allow glimpses of the ducks and cows belonging to the neighboring farm. All these notations are affirmative, signifying heritage, rootedness, and rural community. That the *wych* in wych-elm should sound like *witch* is a serendipitous touch, for Mrs. Wilcox's world is in many ways a counter-Enlightenment world in which superstitions, such as the one about the curative power of the pig's teeth embedded in the tree's trunk, persist, and not everything has to be "productive." Howards End and the neighboring farm resemble, on a smaller scale, Donwell Abbey and the Abbey-mill farm in Jane Austen's *Emma* (1816). In both novels there is the approval of a traditional rural world in which house and farm, garden and meadow, gentry and yeoman (in *Emma*) or yeoman and farmer (in *Howards End*), are interconnected. In both novels, too, there is a troubled awareness of a society in the process of economic transition from a communal structure to a capitalist one.

During Margaret's visit to Howards End, Mr. Wilcox provides her with "the history of the little estate" (214). Fifty years before it had been larger—thirty acres as compared with the present six. Had money been applied, "[o]ne could have made something out of it then—a small park, or at all events shrubberies, and rebuilt the house further away from the road" (214). Henry sounds here like another fictional Henry—Henry Crawford in Jane Austen's *Mansfield Park*, who plans to gentrify Thornton Lacey, another modest country residence. Like Crawford, Henry Wilcox views a house as a commodity reflecting his social status (house and garden becoming what sociologists call "positional goods"), and he recognizes (not unreasonably in a period of agricultural depression) that "the days for small farms are over." Most of the land to the west, Henry points out, "belongs to the people at the Park—they made their pile over copper—good chaps" (214).

Despite Forster's negative view of this engrossment of the land by imperialists, he recognizes that without the infusion of capital there would be no Howards End to describe or value. Indeed, at this point in the novel (chapter 24), the location at Howards End of a connection between the past and the future through the impending marriage of Henry (the no-nonsense capitalist who makes his money in West Africa) and Margaret (the progressive and humanitarian liberal intellectual) seems very possible. Margaret, who has previously learned that Tom Howard, Mrs. Wilcox's soldier brother, was killed in a war and that the two remaining Howard women were unable to keep the place going, recognizes that Henry has saved Howards End. Henry's description of his intervention is of some interest as a textual fragment: "When I had more control I . . . sold off the two and a half animals, and the mangy pony, and the superannuated tools; pulled down the outhouses; drained; thinned out I don't know how many guelder roses and elder trees; and inside the house I turned the old kitchen into a hall, and made the kitchen behind where the dairy was" (214–15).

Clearly, there are negative notes here (Margaret recognizes Henry's lack of "fine feelings or deep insight"); but equally clearly, Henry's words describe the energetic actions needed to reverse a condition of cultural deterioration. In this respect they recall a number of descriptions in English novels in which a worthy but neglected estate is saved from loss by a timely intervention. In Tobias Smollett's *Humphry*

Clinker (1771), for example, Mr. Dennison takes his own deteriorating estate in hand and turns it into a profitable concern: "The floors were repaired, the sashes new glazed. . . . The court-yard was cleared of weeds and rubbish . . . ; bricklayers were set at work upon the barn and stable; and labourers engaged to restore the fences, and begin the work of hedging and ditching."[9] The respect that Margaret extends to Henry's account of his improvements promises a rapprochement between past traditions, based in a rural community, and present behaviors, based in an urban world that obeys the dictates of the financial market. But the promise is not fulfilled. True, Henry and Margaret do marry, and Henry is at Howards End at the novel's close. But by then Henry is a shattered figure; with Howards End in Margaret's possession and bequeathed to Leonard's son, Forster seems unwilling to accommodate Wilcox qualities—except in severely weakened ways—in his social ideal.

The diminution of Henry's vigor, and the marginalization of Howards End as a figure for "England," have long been controversial aspects of the novel, and they will require further comment. Here I merely argue that they are the consequences of a fictional setting (Howards End) and a motif (improvements), and that Forster has not so much painted himself into a corner as followed out the promises of themes deposited in the first chapter of the novel.

Helen's letters show that Mr. Wilcox and the Wilcox children are out of place, as indicated (perhaps too obviously) by their hay fever affliction. Mrs. Wilcox, in contrast, returns from the meadow to the lawn, trailing "her long dress over the sopping grass" and smelling the newly cut hay she has gathered, not to feed the rabbits, as Helen assumes, but to enact for the reader's benefit a connection with nature that is absent in her husband and children. Their disconnection from the traditional rural world is further signified by Helen's report that they are "keen on all games" (4). Like Lytton Strachey in his portrait of Thomas Arnold in *Eminent Victorians* (1918), Forster was critical of the emphasis that the public schools, beginning in the Victorian period, had placed on games, seeing this as one cause of the undeveloped heart of Englishmen.[10] He was also aware of the new social importance that games had acquired in the Edwardian period. The interest that Charles and Evie take in lawn tennis and golf makes them typical of a period in which these games (as Galsworthy's novels also make clear) were becoming the preferred leisure activities of the middle classes, who found them more to their taste (and less expensive) than the traditional field sports of hunting and shooting. Somewhat later in America, William Faulkner provided his version of the theme in *The Sound and the Fury* (1929), where the decline of the Compsons and their traditional world is marked by the golf course carved from their property. True, in *Howards End* the Wilcox men also shoot grouse and fish—indications of their prosperous upper-middle-class status and social aspirations. But the novel's stress is on golf, cricket, and tennis; it is not the least indication of just how far Margaret is willing to go in her attempts to connect with Mr. Wilcox and his world that she should countenance the construction of no fewer than four tennis courts at their planned future house at Midhurst in Sussex (274). The extent of her compromise is further evident in the plans for the house, which is to be much closer to the sort of house Helen and Margaret had originally imagined Howards End to be; Margaret tells Dolly, "We are to have a good many gables and a picturesque skyline" (275).

Forster's dislike of games is also a dislike of the public-school ideal of robust manhood and of the use of this ideal in the service of the Empire. At Oniton, Margaret witnesses Charles and Albert Fussell stymied in their attempt to take a morning swim by the absence of a springboard: "[T]hese athletes seemed paralysed. They could not bathe without their appliances, though the morning sun was calling and the last mists were rising from the dimpling stream. Had they found the life of the body after all?" (228).

Evie Wilcox is very much her brothers' sister. When Margaret goes to Simpson's in the Strand, she sees Evie "staring fiercely at nothing after the fashion of athletic women" (158); earlier, at Howards End, Helen describes how Evie has attached to the greengage tree in the garden a machine on which she does "calisthenic exercises" (4). Women of the time were evidently invited to participate in the robust ideal. In the 1890s Sir George Sitwell told his daughter Edith that "there is nothing a man likes so much as a girl who is good at the parallel bars."[11]

Evie is often the butt of Forster's criticism. Her hobby of breeding puppies to which she gives the names of "the less successful characters of Old Testament history" (148) not only measures her distance from intellectual or cultural interests but is a private joke on Forster's part. As Oliver Stallybrass points out in his note to the Abinger edition, Evie's puppies Ahab and Jezebel are named after characters whose dogs either lick the blood of, or actually eat, their dead owners. In a manuscript draft, Forster had a "greatly daring Evie" name a kitten Ananias. Ananias sells his property but keeps back part of the price; when Peter upbraids him for lying to God, Ananias falls down dead (Acts 5:1–6). Like Ananias, the Wilcoxes are not always scrupulous in their property dealings, as Margaret finds out with respect to both Oniton and Howards End.

Of more interest, however, is the rock garden that Evie creates at Howards End and stocks with alpine plants. Rockeries were common in Edwardian gardens; H. J. Bidder's rock garden at St. John's College, Oxford, was famous. In 1908 Reginald Farrer published *Alpines and Bog Plants*, and in 1909 *My Rock Garden*. Evie's hobby is therefore fashionable, and this is in part what is wrong with it: like the greenhouse that John Dashwood secures for his wife at Norland Park in *Sense and Sensibility*—which requires the cutting down of some old walnut trees—the rock garden is a status marker and is ill suited in scale or purpose to the place. It is also likely to have been expensive; Farrer himself recognized that "the very rich are out to purchase the glories of the Alps at so much a yard."[12] And a final mark in its disfavor in this often chauvinistic novel: its plants are not English.

An even more intrusive item in the garden is the motorcar. In London—where, like her biblical namesake, she is sick for home amid the alien corn[13]—Ruth Wilcox tells Margaret of the garage that her husband has recently built "to the west of the house, not far from the wych-elm, in what used to be the paddock for the pony" (74). Mr. Wilcox, during his conversation with Margaret on the Chelsea Embankment, describes how they "messed away with a garage all among the wych-elm roots" (141–42).

Forster's antagonism to the motorcar is consistent in *Howards End*, and problematic. When Charles meets Mrs. Munt at the Hilton station, he drives her to Howards End, stopping on the way to contemplate "the cloud of dust that they had raised in their passage through the village. . . . Some of it had percolated through the open windows, some had whitened the roses and the gooseberries of the wayside gardens, while a certain proportion had entered the lungs of the villagers. 'I wonder when they'll learn wisdom and tar the roads,' was his comment" (18–19).

In fact, just at the time *Howards End* was being composed, the government had responded to the major problems of dust and mud resulting from motorcar traffic. Lloyd George in his "people's budget" of 1909 had created the Road Board, which was to raise a sum of £600,000 from special taxes on petrol and motor licenses, for the tarring of the roads. In R. C. K. Ensor's opinion, the Road Board proved to be "an unqualified national boon."[14] In this context, Forster's criticism of the automobile may indicate a politically regressive attitude, a sign of his inability to negotiate with a world irreversibly launched toward a technological future. In the environment-conscious 1990s, however, I am more inclined to see Forster as a prophet of our present ecological anxieties.

Forster's criticism of the motorcar has meaning for the present but was not in itself a scientific criticism; rather, Forster viewed the motorcar as the most prominent sign of a modernity that was losing its connection with a communal and moral heritage—that was dominating rather than living with nature. In the process, it was altering the way people thought: the new speed of travel prevented them from appreciating the countryside. The motorcar runs through the novel like the car of Juggernaut: it is an instrument of destruction. Margaret is prevented from visiting Howards End with Mrs. Wilcox when Evie suddenly appears at King's Cross to explain why she and her father have returned from Yorkshire: "No—motor smash—changed plans— father's coming." The smash, her father adds (also in staccato speech), was with "a wretched horse and cart" (90). Later, on the trip to Evie's wedding, the car driven by Charles hits and kills a cat, and when Charles refuses to stop at her request, Margaret jumps out of the car, cutting her hand. Her action is a protest against the impersonality of a modern (gesellschaft) life in which payments by insurance companies have replaced the human contacts of a more communal (gemeinschaft) world. After the affair is settled, Margaret reflects: "No doubt she had disgraced herself. But she felt their whole journey from London had been unreal. They had no part with the earth and its emotions. They were dust, and a stink, and cosmopolitan chatter, and the girl whose cat had been killed had lived more deeply than they" (223–24).

Forster's antagonism toward the motorcar resembles the distrust of technology that is found in D. H. Lawrence's novels and stories. In *Howards End*, it is not only the instinctual life of the body that Forster sets against a dehumanizing technology, but the vanishing world of the rural past—the world, that is, for which Howards End and the Hertfordshire countryside provide the metonymic expression. In her second letter, Helen describes how Charles takes them out every day in the motorcar; in describing the landscape through which he drives (too quickly for the eye to take it all in), Helen unwittingly provides a critical perspective: ". . . a tomb with trees in it, a hermit's house, a wonderful road that was made by the Kings of Mercia—tennis—a cricket match—bridge—and at night we squeeze up in this lovely house" (5–6).

Thus, already in the first chapter, with its thematic attention to games, gardens, and garages, the difficulties of connection are posed to the reader (if not quite yet to Helen) as the frenetic and philistine activities of the Wilcoxes are played out against the backdrop of an immemorial past.

Only in Mrs. Wilcox are the values of the past still present—and useful in dissolving moments of crisis, as when Charles angrily confronts Paul over his apparent engagement to Helen. Demanding "a plain answer," Charles is checked by the arrival of his mother: "She seemed to belong not to the young people and their motor, but to the house, and to the tree that overshadowed it. One knew that she worshipped the past, and that the instinctive wisdom that the past can alone bestow had descended upon her. . . . High-born she might not be. But assuredly she cared about her ancestors, and let them help her" (22–23).

Forster's sentiments here (for the "one knew" attaches to him, not to the imperceptive Mrs. Munt, the nominal observer of the scene) resemble those of Edmund Burke in his *Reflections on the Revolution in France* (1790). There is the same trust that the customary habits of the past may become so ingrained in human nature as to act as instinctive moral guides in the present. To invoke Burke is, of course, to note also the distance between his militant conservatism, which rested on a belief in the interdependence of politics and religion, and Forster's far more diffident conservatism, which, like Mrs. Wilcox's "gentle conservatism" (96), lacked both political and religious conviction. Forster's quiet tributes to Howards End are hardly the equivalent of Burke's sublime paean to Windsor Castle, which becomes, in *A Letter to a Noble Lord* (1796), a figure for a constitutional monarchy old and powerful enough to withstand the onslaught of revolutionary zeal. But it is worth observing that Forster, too, can sound the trumpet of Shakespearean chauvinism (as in his descriptions in chapter 19 of the scene from the summits of the Purbeck Hills), and that he uses Howards End in Burkean ways to oppose a modern world whose secular and rational attitudes separate it from sustaining traditions, which carry a kind of spiritual consecration.

No less than Burke, Forster is open to the charge of committing what Jeremy Bentham called "the wisdom-of-our-ancestors fallacy."[15] By making the Wilcoxes Benthamites, however, Forster qualifies the force of utilitarian objections to a Burkean insistence that history be made part of the human equation. Like Evie attaching her machine to the greengage tree, the Wilcoxes "put everything to use" (4); but like Charles "messing away" at the roots of the wych-elm tree to build his garage, they injure in the process a culturally sustaining heritage. Their way of reacting to crisis is very different from Mrs. Wilcox's. When they learn of her bequest of Howards End to Margaret, they respond coolly, analytically, and selfishly. Forster's narrator acquits them on legal grounds, commenting: "To them Howards End was a house: they could not know that to her it had been a spirit, for which she sought a spiritual heir. . . . Is it credible that the possessions of the spirit can be bequeathed at all? . . . A wych-elm tree, a vine, a wisp of hay with dew on it—can passion for such things be transmitted where there is no bond of blood?" (103).

The novel's answer is yes. Margaret, denied her legacy following the funeral, receives it as a gift from her husband at the end of the novel; but long before this she has shown that she is the best heir. During her first visit to Howards End, she finds the door of the house unexpectedly open and, while Henry is away looking for the key, enters it. Henry's lack of a key is less a sign of his sexual inadequacy than of his noncommunication with the traditional past; Margaret has also to show him the pig's teeth in the tree. As she wanders through the house, it seems to reverberate, and when she flings open the door to the upstairs:

> A noise as of drums seemed to deafen her. A woman, an old woman, was descending, with figure erect, with face impassive, with lips that parted and said dryly:
> "Oh! Well, I took you for Ruth Wilcox."
> Margaret stammered: "I—Mrs. Wilcox—I?"
> "In fancy, of course—in fancy. You had her way of walking. Good day." And the old woman passed out into the rain. (211)

Forster's gothic crescendo (the drums recalling the drums in Beethoven's Fifth) is very effective in suggesting a spiritual transmission of values from Mrs. Wilcox to Miss Avery (who for a second seems to be Mrs. Wilcox's ghost) to Margaret (whom Miss Avery takes for Mrs. Wilcox, and who will shortly become the second Mrs. Wilcox). "I—Mrs. Wilcox—I" is Forster's symbolic shorthand for the change that occurs in Margaret's identity as a consequence of Mrs. Wilcox's entry into her life and consciousness.

Miss Avery, described by Wilfred Stone as "an old crone," is a touchstone of value in the novel.[16] Friend of Mrs. Wilcox and her Howard grandmother, proposed to by Tom Howard (who was killed in a war), condescended to by Evie (who crudely refuses her gift of an expensive wedding present), tolerated by Henry Wilcox only "because he could get good value" out of her (278), considered by Dolly to be a dotty old maid—Miss Avery represents the integrity and charity of an older world before the inception of class consciousness and possessive individualism. The Howards, she tells Margaret, were "a very civil family. Old Mrs. Howard never spoke against anybody, nor let anyone be turned away without food. Then it was never 'Trespassers will be prosecuted' in their land, but would people please not come in?" (286–87). Ruth Howard, she adds, should have married a soldier.

On first-name terms with Mrs. Wilcox during her life, Miss Avery is Mrs. Wilcox's posthumous surrogate in the episode of Margaret's first visit to Howards End; she also recalls Mrs. Wilcox's early response to Charles's anger when, at the climax of the novel, she alone recognizes that he has killed Leonard and says with sibylline finality, "Yes, murder's enough" (340). Earlier, on Margaret's second visit to Howards End—the visit necessitated by Miss Avery's unauthorized laying out of the Schlegel books and furniture in the house—Miss Avery is again Mrs. Wilcox's representative, insisting through her words and actions, correctly as it turns out, that Margaret will come to live at Howards End rather than build the new house at Midhurst.

In the details of his description of Margaret's visit, Forster provides a coded criticism of Wilcoxite capitalism. On her walk with Miss Avery, Margaret sees that the garden has grown wild, the gravel sweep has become weedy, grass has "sprung up at the very jaws of the garage," and all that remains of Evie's rockery is bumps (285). In returning Howards End to its earlier condition, Forster repeats a common structure in conservative fiction. To cite *Humphry Clinker* again: Matthew Bramble reverses the false improvements made to Baynard's estate by his wife (whose fortune, not incidentally, comes from city sources): "The shrubbery is condemned to extirpation; and the pleasure ground . . . restored to its original use of corn-field and pasture."[17]

In chapter 40, when Helen and Margaret stay the night at Howards End, Miss Avery "crossed the lawn and merged into the hedge that divided it from the farm. An old gap, which Mr. Wilcox had filled up, had reappeared, and her track through the dew followed the path that he had turfed over when he improved the garden and made it possible for games" (329). As Miss Avery literally retraces the first Mrs. Wilcox's footsteps, the connection between house and farm, closed by Henry's improvements, opens up again; it remains open at the end when Helen and Margaret are described as "sitting on the remains of Evie's rockery, where the lawn merged into the field" (351), while Tom, the farmer's boy, plays in the hay with Helen's child. In the end is the novel's beginning. Once more it is haytime—for the Wilcoxes, the season of hay fever—and the red poppies that Mrs. Wilcox watched come out, as reported in Helen's first letter, are reopening in the garden. After the bitterness and the tragedy, after Helen's pregnancy, Henry's vicious reaction, Charles's anger, and Leonard's death, the persons of the drama achieve peace and happiness in a pastoral setting in which—to recall Bachelard's useful word—anthropocosmic ties have been reestablished. During the last chapter, the farmer mows the meadow, "encompassing with narrowing circles the sacred centre of the field" (350), and at the end: " 'The field's cut!' Helen cried excitedly—'the big meadow! We've seen to the very end, and it'll be such a crop of hay as never!' " (359).

For Forster, as for T. S. Eliot in *Burnt Norton* (1935), "home is where one starts from," and as in Eliot's poem so in Forster's conclusion: the laughter of children in the garden suggests spiritual possibilities. In another comparison, the "joy" (359) of the novel's conclusion perhaps authorizes us to hear echoes of Schiller's "Ode to Joy," sung in Beethoven's Ninth Symphony ("*Alle Menschen werden Brüder*"). "In these English farms," Margaret had thought earlier, silently citing Schiller and Arnold, "one might see life steadily and see it whole, group in one vision its transitoriness and its eternal youth, connect—connect without bitterness until all men are brothers" (281).

Impressed as we may be by the novel's closing affirmation, we may yet wonder about its political meaning.[18] For Forster, any solution to the social and political fragmentation of the Edwardian world had to involve a (re)connection with the values metonymically represented by Howards End. Considered as a structure of representation, Howards End suggests a conservative, rather than liberal system of values, one that is resistant to the "improvements" of utilitarian and predatory capitalists. Yet its continuing presence in the landscape is the consequence of the reparative action of a liberal imperialist; hence, perhaps, Forster's inclusion of Henry, however weakened, in the final scene. Howards End is evidently more accommodating, however, to the progressive liberalism represented—in different ways—by the Schlegel sisters. Does Howards End—house and novel—need men at all? (Angrily facing Henry and Dr. Mansbridge, Margaret tells them, "I do not need you in the least," as she reunites with Helen at the end of chapter 36 [304].) Even to ask this question might seem to give support to the negative verdicts of Stone and Crews—to Stone's argument that Forster has sacrificed his Red-Bloods to his Mollycoddles, or to Crews's view that Forster's novel "ends by crushing society on the altar of the private life."[19] But a consideration of Forster's use of the novel of manners—and in particular, of the marriage plot on which that genre depends—may show that *Howards End* is not a reprehensible retreat from politics but a radical critique of politics as it appears domestically in relationships between the sexes and the classes. To the novel's characters, and particularly the Schlegel sisters, then, it is time to turn.

7

Characters

The great thing in the book is the sisters' affection for each other;
personal relationships, except those between lovers, have never . . .
been made more beautiful or more real.
  —Unsigned review of *Howards End, Athenaeum* (1910)

That the affection of sisters should be the central value in the novel
makes it unusual, as I shall argue in a moment, but in other respects—
its realism, its restricted range of characters, its domestic focus, and
its interest in money—*Howards End* is typical of the novel of manners.
Like Jane Austen, who advised a novel-writing niece that "three or
four families in a country village is the very thing to work on," Forster
conceived of society in familial contexts.[1] Ruth Wilcox, her husband
Henry, and their three children, Charles, Paul, and Evie; the Schlegel
sisters, Margaret and Helen, and their brother Tibby; Leonard Bast
and his wife Jacky—these three groups, each assigned an appropriate
milieu, and each accompanied by a satellite cast of secondary characters (again, few in number), essentially compose the characterization
of the novel. Even for a novel of manners, the cast is small. Does this
fact, and the novel's domestic focus, limit the power of Forster's social
criticism?

Only once do we (along with Margaret) see Henry Wilcox at his
place of work, the Imperial and West African Rubber Company. We
never see Leonard slaving away at the Porphyrion or at Dempster's
Bank, and as for the Schlegels, their unearned incomes assure them a

"life of cultured but not ignoble ease" (112). Work as a fact of life is as conspicuous by its absence from the novel as it is by its absence from *Aspects of the Novel*, where Forster, in his chapter "People," claims that "the main facts in human life are five: birth, food, sleep, love and death."[2]

The omission of work in the above list seems more blatant than the omission of money, for money is a central concern in *Howards End*. "Money pads the edges of things," Margaret recognizes, adding that "the lowest abyss is not the absence of love, but the absence of coin" (62–63). And in what follows, Forster specifies how far from the abyss the Schlegels are: Tibby has £800 a year, and Margaret and Helen £600 each. To get a sense of the middle-class comfort these figures represent, we need only recall the inheritance, guaranteeing £500 a year, that released Virginia Woolf's narrator in *A Room of One's Own* (1929) from a life of drudgery, or the £250 a year that, as Woolf angrily asserted in *Three Guineas* (1938), was all that many professional women earned in the 1930s. Within the novel itself, the purchasing power of the pound in the Edwardian period is shown when Helen doubts the wisdom of having "spent a matter of eight pounds" on the Basts (244); with this sum, it seems, she has paid their arrears in rent, redeemed their furniture, provided them with dinner and breakfast, and bought their (and her own) train tickets from London to Shrewsbury.

Forster is less specific about the incomes of the Wilcoxes and the Basts, but we learn that Mr. Wilcox is not far from being a millionaire (139), and that the ruin of the Basts is hastened by Helen's neglecting to pay their hotel bill at Oniton. Leonard's income as a clerk, even at the Porphyrion, probably would not greatly exceed the annual rent of £120 that the Wilcoxes pay for their London flat, and it would fall well short of the £300 per annum that Margaret proposes as a generous disposal of the hypothetical millionaire's charity to poor individuals, during the debate at the informal discussion club in chapter 15. After the disastrous Oniton encounter Helen wants to give £5,000 to the Basts. Tibby objects that this is nearly half of her principal. Helen denies it, pointing out that such a sum will realize £150; at the same 3 percent, her £600 a year signifies a fortune of £20,000. With such details Forster measures Leonard's penury and gives poignancy to his conversation with Helen, when, all cultural aspirations abandoned, he sees that money underlies all human activities (chapter 27). Unlike Miss Avery, Leonard could hardly afford a "lovely enamel pendant" costing £5 from a Bond Street jeweler; as it is, Evie decides that Miss Avery's wedding gift is too expensive to accept "from a farm-woman" (277).

Forster never lets us forget that character and cash are interdependent considerations. "You and I and the Wilcoxes stand upon money as upon islands," Margaret informs Mrs. Munt, adding (as if she had recently read Marx) that "the very soul of the world is economic" (63). On more than one occasion—and despite a general distrust of social movement that she shares with her creator—Margaret is grateful for the mobility that money permits, glad of the opportunity, unavailable to the poor, simply to leave displeasing people or an awkward situation, by going on a European holiday or moving to a house in the country (66, 117). Unlike Henry, who "winces" at her frankness on the subject of money and marriage settlements ("How much have you a year?" she asks him. "I've six hundred" [188]), Margaret wishes to bring the subject of money into the open; she considers money to be "the warp of civilization, whatever the woof may be" (133).

In such instances she surely speaks for Forster who, himself the beneficiary of a modest legacy from his great-aunt (£8,000), was both grateful for and somewhat guilty about his unearned income. Even when, later in life, he made a lot of money from royalties, Forster's attitude toward money was unusual; he gave considerable sums to individuals (thus agreeing with Margaret's views on charity); but he also left large sums in his current account, declining to make money from money. Margaret's intention at the end of *Howards End* (announced by Henry) "to diminish her income by half during the next ten years" (357) foreshadows the actual behavior of Forster, who left at his death an estate of $151,000 to his literary executor, with King's College as the final legatee.[3] Doubtless, the bequest would have been larger had he, too, not systematically reduced his income over the years.

Margaret's frankness about money is refreshing, but it is the frankness of the enlightened middle-class liberal intellectual whose pronouncements, precisely because she herself is not financially embarrassed, must often sound theoretical. It is as unfair to blame Forster for not imagining poverty from poverty's point of view, however, as it is to blame him for not showing his characters at work. Forster had no inside knowledge of the world of business at either Mr. Wilcox's or Leonard Bast's level, and he wisely stayed within the range of his novelist's eye and ear. What he possessed was a knowledge of middle-class life in its domestic aspects. As in Austen's novels, however, a microhistorical focus has macrohistorical implications. From manners he moves, beyond morals, to politics. Forster is not a Scott or a Stendhal or a Tolstoy, introducing world-historical figures into *Howards End*. But his characters—especially Margaret, who disdains "the heroic outfit" (191)—have the typicality that Georg Lukács admired in realistic fiction: they are at once living, breathing individuals and representative types—characters whose inner being, as well as outer speech and actions, derives from the pressures of the historical moment.[4]

True, as a comic novelist, Forster also creates secondary, "stock" characters—types in a Theophrastan rather than Lukácsian sense. Thus, Mrs. Munt, though she typifies an Edwardian philistine and chauvinist, is a comic turn as interfering aunt; and the German cousins, though they represent German nationalism of the time, are also "stage" Germans, absurdly literal and humorless. A cockney staginess attaches to Jacky also, and the primary figure of Leonard—as Forster has him speak and act—is much less convincing than the middle-class Schlegels and Wilcoxes, with whose milieu Forster was intimately familiar. Even less "real," as already discussed, is Hamar Bryce, a narrative function masquerading as a character.

Inheriting a genre that typically uses the marriage plot to cross social as well as sexual divisions, Forster sought to make its conventions serve his own purposes. From their "backwater" in Wickham Place, the Schlegel sisters make forays into the practical world of men: Helen, after the failure of her connection with Paul, travels downward (socially) to her momentary sexual union (born of sympathy) with

Leonard; Margaret travels upward to her enduring union (rational rather than passionate) with Henry. Yet Leonard dies, Henry is debilitated at the end, Margaret does not want children, Helen will never marry. As a novel of manners, *Howards End* ends oddly, its resolution qualified by the fact that the convincing union is not between a man and a woman but between sisters.

Forster's affirmation of female friendship has more radical import than his critical treatment of the individual marriages in *Howards End*. The novel of manners typically anatomizes imperfect matrimonial unions as it develops an ideal marriage—"the real thing," which, as in Tom Stoppard's 1982 play with this title, redeems marriage as an institution even as it affirms romantic love as a value. Forster, too, gives us a number of imperfect marriages—but without the corrective ideal. The first Mrs. Wilcox's marriage to Henry was hardly one of true minds and seems to have been undertaken to save Howards End from ruin; more troubling, Ruth Wilcox's spiritual qualities have not descended to her children. Charles, the bully and motorcar enthusiast, marries Dolly, who has "one of those triangular faces that so often prove attractive to a robust man" (73). Described as breeding like rabbits, Charles and Dolly increase the population of the imperialists who are supplanting the yeomen and changing England for the worse. In the service of imperialism, Paul, who might have married Helen, leaves for Africa, remains unmarried, and becomes a coarse and brutal figure. Evie the athlete, meanwhile, marries Percy Cahill, Dolly's uncle and a man old enough to be her father. At a lower social level, the marriage of Leonard and Jacky is a squalid and barren affair.

It may be that Forster discovered in and through the writing of *Howards End* that a conventional marriage plot, far from expressing a positive social vision, would only perpetuate the social conventions making for oppression and disconnection. That he did not start the novel with this recognition, however, is suggested by his notebook journal entry for 31 December 1907: "Have been strongly attracted . . . to acquiescence in social conventions, economic trend,—efficiency—and see that others may do right to acquiesce and that I may do wrong to laugh at them, and that great art was never a conscious rebel."[5] But even as (in the same entry) Forster announces his intention to write a more positive and accommodating novel than *The Longest Journey*—which had attacked conventional society, satirized the "efficiency" promoted by public schools, and placed male friendship above marriage—he also reveals the gulf between his world and the conventional world. "There is no doubt," he wrote, "that I do not resemble other people, and even they notice it." Though Forster seems not to have fully acknowledged his homosexuality until his encounter in 1913 with Edward Carpenter and George Merrill at Millthorpe, he knew from a much earlier time that he was "a minority, if not a solitary."[6] Unlike *Maurice*, finished in 1914 but not published until after his death, *Howards End* is not an overtly homosexual novel. Neither is it covertly so; one looks in vain here for male friendships like that between Philip and Gino in *Where Angels Fear to Tread*, or between Rickie and Ansell in *The Longest Journey*, or between Fielding and Aziz in *A Passage to India*—friendships whose final in-completion is at once a criticism of English society and a refusal, however unconscious, to acquiesce in a system that finds no place for homosexual love.

In several respects, *Howards End* is the most conventional of Forster's novels, a fact that may account for D. H. Lawrence's criticism in a 1922 letter: "But I think you *did* make a nearly deadly mistake glorifying those *business* people in *Howards End*. Business is no good."[7] Critics have more often faulted Forster for sacrificing the Wilcoxes than for "glorifying" them, yet Lawrence's remarks find justification in the text of *Howards End*. No less than Margaret, Forster wanted to do justice to his business people and the robust and masculine life they led: "She could not despise it, as Helen and Tibby affected to do. It fostered such virtues as neatness, decision and obedience, virtues of the second rank, no doubt, but they have formed our civilization" (108). Later, Margaret insists to Helen that, without the Wilcox spirit, "there would be no trains, no ships to carry us literary people about in, no fields even" (183).

In a less direct way the character of Tibby provides support for Lawrence's opinion. Detached, aesthetic, cynical, and selfish, Tibby may well be a vehicle for Forster's self-criticism. Not at all like Thoby Stephen, he more resembles the languid reclining figure of James Strachey in Duncan Grant's 1909 portrait (in the Tate Gallery).[8] With his unearned income, he (like Forster) need follow no profession, but his disdain for the professions is not at all approved in the novel. His "bleat" (114) irritates both his sisters, who call him "Tibbikins" and, on one occasion, "Auntie Tibby" (44). At Wickham Place, when he is not sick or suffering from hay fever, Tibby's chief interest is in brands of tea; at Oxford he adds a casual interest in scholarship to his solitary, epicurean life. Forster redeems Tibby to some extent: he may be selfish, but he is not cruel: though affected, he never poses. But his treatment of Helen on her arrival from Oniton is cold and unsympathetic. In chapter 13 he is the object of Margaret's criticism when she disparages one of his friends—Mr. Vyse, the aesthetic snob who has wandered into *Howards End* from *A Room with a View*—as "rather a wretched, weedy man" (114). She mentions another friend: "Guy. That was a pitiful business" (114). "That," we may assume, was a scandal involving homosexuality. In these ways, Tibby is presented as the opposite of the Wilcox men (while Tibby is deciding against Orange Pekoe, Paul Wilcox is outfitting himself for his career in Africa), and Tibby's "Oxford" dilettantism and "leisure without sympathy" (324) appear unfavorably against the Wilcoxes' ideology of work, duty, and Empire—an ideology that Margaret, surprisingly, defends. She is driven to this position by Tibby's effeminacy, a characteristic that may also have led her to interview Tibby's riding master (75). But her attitude, plainly, is in the service of Forster's "conventional" aims.

In Margaret's view, Wickham Place is a "female house": ". . . it must be feminine, and all we can do is to see that it isn't effeminate. Just as another house that I can mention, but won't, sounded irrevocably masculine, and all its inmates can do is to see that it isn't brutal" (45). In this spectrum of sexuality (effeminacy-femininity-masculinity-brutality), Forster suggests that a normative human mean is achievable through the marriage of a woman and a man, respectively divested of their less desirable gender traits. Margaret and Henry, at this point, seem likely candidates for a union that will enact an ideal vision of society. Even after Jacky's exposure of Henry's infidelity, Margaret can shift from thinking that the sexes are separate races and their love "a mere device of Nature's to keep things going" to a more idealistic conception of heterosexual union: "She knew that out of Nature's device we have built a magic that will win us immortality. Far more mysterious than the call of sex to sex is the tenderness that we throw into that call" (252). Though such idealism recurs in the novel, *Howards End* finally reveals Forster to be less interested in normalizing definitions of masculinity and femininity than in exploring the way in which both terms are the constructions of a particular time and place. Whereas the novel, on occasions, seems to be striving for a natural stability of sexuality, based in a received logic of binary oppositions, on other occasions it comes close to saying that such stability is a patriarchal myth. Great art, in Forster's notebook phrase, may not be a conscious rebel; in the instance of *Howards End*, however, may it unconsciously be so?

The answer, I believe, is yes, but the nature and extent of Forster's rebellion are not easy to describe. As I have proposed in chapter 4, *Howards End* is not a "work" in which characters, plot, theme, and language act together to produce a determinate final vision. With respect to both sexuality and social conventions, the novel sends contradictory signals. Even so, a critique of existing sexual and social standards emerges, and we can best describe this critique if we evaluate the relations—oppositional and conciliatory, respectively—that Helen and Margaret have with the Wilcoxes.

The first chapter presents us with an immediate connection, in the Helen-Paul affair, between the world of the intelligentsia and the world of business. Helen's three letters to Margaret—vivacious, intelligent, enthusiastic—describe her week's visit to Howards End, where, even before she falls in love with Paul, she falls in love generally with the family: "The energy of the Wilcoxes had fascinated her . . . she had *liked* being told that her notions of life were sheltered or academic; that Equality was nonsense, Votes for Women nonsense, Socialism nonsense, Art and Literature, except when conducive to strengthening the character, nonsense" (24). But Helen's connection with the Wilcoxes is a spurious connection, made at the cost of her personal and political convictions. She even resolves to be less polite to servants in future. Only briefly, however. At breakfast, following the evening of Paul's kiss beneath the wych-elm tree, she is suddenly aware of her error, and her impulsive attraction to the Wilcoxes is succeeded by an equal and opposite revulsion. She decides the whole family is a fraud, "just a wall of newspapers and motor-cars and golf-clubs," with nothing behind it but "panic and emptiness" (26). She sends a telegram, saying "all is over." What follows in chapter 3 is a comedy of cross-purposes between Aunt Juley and Charles Wilcox, in which Charles reveals himself to be more "brutal" than "masculine," if not quite the Conradian hollow man of Helen's imagination.

While Helen, the sister of "sensibility," meets and recoils from the Wilcoxes at Howards End, Margaret, the sister of "sense," makes a more gradual rapprochement with the family. After an initial faux pas, she befriends Mrs. Wilcox in London, and after Mrs. Wilcox's death, her chance meeting with Mr. Wilcox on the Chelsea Embankment leads to their engagement and, despite the later revelation of his sordid past affair with Jacky, eventual marriage. Her connection with Henry survives his brutal attitude toward Helen's pregnancy and the death of Leonard. On Margaret, then, falls the burden of connection. After her first contact, Helen is consistently hostile to the Wilcoxes. She responds with dismay on the Dorset downs to the news of Margaret's engagement, is incensed when Henry's suggestion that Leonard leave the Porphyrion backfires, and angrily confronts Henry with the Basts at Oniton. After her (failed) attempt to give money to the Basts, Helen leaves England, pregnant with Leonard's child; in Europe, she lives with Monica, a "crude feminist of the South" (307).

Had Forster intended a frontal assault on the social and sexual mores of his time, he might have endorsed Helen's departure and her implied lesbian relationship with Monica. Forster's critique, plainly, did not go this far; in the novel's sexual spectrum, Helen has moved to an extreme. (Despite being the opposite of the Wilcoxes in so many ways, Helen resembles them in others: in her penchant for sending telegrams, for example, and in the growing "brutality" of her opinions

[68].) For Forster's purposes, Helen has to return to Howards End from her European exile; unlike Lawrence and Joyce, Forster sought insular solutions. Yet his critique of social conventions, by way of a critique of sexual conventions, is keen enough in *Howards End*. Helen, who "used to be so dreamy about a man's love," at the end has given up on romantic love as an ideal (353). And Margaret, for much of the novel the agent of Forster's "conventional" intentions, has changed also.

Helen, as a voice of social criticism, is an ambivalent and vulnerable character. Her impulsive nature, absolute judgments, black-and-white morality, and volatile temperament all make the quality of her social concern problematic. Like Austen in *Sense and Sensibility*, however, Forster never allows his younger heroine to forfeit our sympathies entirely. Even so, Margaret's calmer nature, more conciliatory attitudes, and socially more positive actions give her a greater claim to being Forster's spokesperson in the novel.

Forster skillfully shapes the pattern of the sisters' temporary separation and eventual reunion. The breach begins to open in chapter 22, as Margaret seeks to help her "lord" build "the rainbow bridge that should connect the prose in us with the passion" (194). In this passage, Margaret's thoughts are the vehicle of Forster's Freudian essay on the difficulties modern middle-class males have with the expression of their sexual desire. Taught to view bodily passion as bad, they cannot love their wives without shame; but incompletely ascetic, they seek sexual release elsewhere, as, we learn later, Henry did with Jacky. Margaret's mood is high: "Only connect!" (195). In bringing his novel's epigraph into the novel and into Margaret's consciousness, Forster replaces the ellipsis points with an exclamation point, as if to emphasize Margaret's confidence that she can reconcile the "monk" and the "beast" in Henry's psyche. But then, as if to adumbrate the less optimistic mood of the novel's conclusion, the narrator reveals that Margaret's "sermon" has failed in its purpose.

The reason for failure is quickly evident in Henry's brutal disregard for the personal values that the sisters hold sacrosanct. The issue is Leonard's departure from the Porphyrion and his employment, at a reduced wage, at Dempster's Bank. As the manuscript page reproduced at the head of chapter 8 shows, Henry's insensitivity is conveyed through a dialogue in which he repeatedly fails to pick up on Margaret's insistent questions. Ignorant of Margaret's concern for Leonard, he is also unaware of Helen's intensifying anger. Despite Margaret's attempts at mediation, Henry's insouciance outrages Helen, who blames Henry (and herself) for Leonard's reduced circumstances. In what follows, it is less important to decide how far Henry is personally responsible (at Oniton, Margaret tells Helen she is wrong to call Henry to account for a chance remark) than it is to evaluate the economic philosophy he gives voice to. In a series of speeches (198–200), Henry provides—as critics have long recognized—a redaction of the arguments of the classical liberal thinkers against the wisdom, and even the morality, of the government's intervention in the economic process. His remarks here and in an earlier conversation (152–53) recall Adam Smith's theories of laissez-faire and the "invisible hand," Thomas Malthus's pessimistic conclusion that without war, famine, and disease population would so increase as to outstrip available resources, David Ricardo's iron law of wages, and Victorian applications of Charles Darwin's theories of natural selection to human affairs. For humanitarian liberals like Helen and Margaret, Henry's "scientific" theories provide a self-serving rationalization for his class's continuing exploitation of the poor. But whereas Helen repudiates Henry's outlook, Margaret still hopes to humanize her future husband. Meanwhile, Henry brusquely overrides her request to honor a family tradition by staying another week with her aunt at The Bays.

The drama of the novel from this point onward centers not on Helen and her absolute repudiation of Henry's inhumane brand of capitalism but on Margaret and her valiant attempts to accept and be accepted in Henry's world. Though these attempts entail compromises and role playing, they are not, initially, hypocritical. She may characterize her "love-making" as "prose" in contrast to the "romance" of Helen's with Paul (182); but she finds Henry sexually attractive and, though in her early thirties, is not marrying merely for convenience. Aware of the differences between their outlooks—he, a utilitarian businessman, sees life "steadily," while she, sensitive to the private and the mysterious, sees it "whole"—she nevertheless likes being with him, pays "homage" to the "robust" type he represents, and, presumably, sees in their union the possibility of Matthew Arnold's ideal of proportion (168–69).[9] Thus, when at Simpson's she allows Henry to choose her meal, or at Ducie Street keeps her criticisms of his furniture to herself, she exhibits tact, not bad faith. If her principles are outraged, she can act, as when on the journey to Oniton she leaps from the moving car to sympathize with the girl whose cat they have run over. To Charles, who had ignored her request to stop, she appears as "a woman in revolt" (223); but with the incident over and her injury proving to be slight, she takes up the "line" that she has been "naughty" (224) and allows Charles and his father to believe that her act represented a typical female failure of nerve.

At Oniton, even as she is secretly critical of Evie's wedding—"a blend of Sunday church and fox-hunting" (232)—she remains hopeful that her own marriage will succeed, and that Henry will be the better for her exercises of tact and love. Henry's house is a "genuine country house," complete with butler, servants, and a wine cellar, and Margaret is determined "to assimilate" the establishment; realizing that "her only ally [is] the power of Home," she intends to "create new sanctities among these hills" (231–32). Regarding her future abode as a special place on the border between England and Wales, Saxon and Celt, she wishes it also to be a place where, the old warfare between monk and beast forgotten, a man and a woman can come together in harmony and social usefulness. To this end, she is anxious "to start straight with the clergy . . . and, if possible, to see something of the local life" (218).

Her quasi-feudal hopes are dashed, but not, it is worth noting, by Helen's angry arrival at Oniton with the Basts and the consequent exposure of Henry's lurid past. Margaret's wish to build the rainbow bridge survives even these revelations; believing Henry's adultery to be the first Mrs. Wilcox's tragedy, she allows him to build up his fortress of self-respect and goes ahead with a quiet wedding. It is only on their honeymoon in Innsbruck that she learns that Henry has, without consulting her, leased Oniton to a school, on account of its drawbacks: the shooting is poor, the fishing indifferent, and besides, it is damp and therefore, as Margaret ironically comments, only fit to be inhabited by little boys. She is not to be its mistress, nor will the Wilcoxes become part of the place: "It is not their names that recur in the parish register. It is not their ghosts that sigh among the alders at evening. They have swept into the valley and swept out of it, leaving a little dust and a little money behind" (261).

Margaret had hoped that her marriage to Henry would be a connection with a historical past—providing, in Burkean fashion, a guide for present conduct—and with a natural world—exercising, in Wordsworthian fashion, a binding force on human character. But Henry's "cosmopolitan" and "nomadic" behavior militates against such connections, even as his personal deficiencies make it unlikely that the kind of love he can offer will be a substitute, in a commercial world, for the sustenance earlier supplied by heritage and nature. These are Margaret's thoughts on learning of the loss of the Oniton house (272–73)—or rather, since the passage is in the *style indirect libre*, these thoughts effectively disqualifying the Wilcoxes as heirs of traditional England are Forster's. Through the unsatisfactory outcome of his marriage plot, Forster opposes the predatory economic individualism of the liberal imperialists. He also exposes the sexual ideology that upholds their world.

Forster reveals the growing strain of Margaret's efforts to "assimilate" Henry's world while retaining her own principles and her sister's love. Aware of prevailing patriarchal constructions of femininity (Henry, for example, is "far from discouraging timidity in females" [211]), Margaret has been willing to play her assigned roles in public, even to the extent of "kow-towing" to the men at the wedding (233). But her role playing becomes more problematic after Helen arrives, "furiously" shouting that she has found the Basts in a starving condition (234). Margaret is properly critical of her sister's "perverted notion of philanthropy" (235), but the question is complicated not so much by her wish to preserve appearances—a reasonable desire, in the circumstances—but by her hostility toward the Basts. Helen rightly resents her description of them as "hangers-on" (235). Moreover, when Margaret tells Leonard, "rather conventionally," that "we would like to find you work" (237), or later, when she sends her curt, dismissive letters to Leonard and Helen, she seems uncharacteristically insensitive. Helen can hardly be blamed for thinking the letters were dictated by Mr. Wilcox.

Margaret's temporary forfeiture of Helen's and the reader's sympathy is partly the consequence of Forster's need to write to his "pattern." To bring about the breach between the sisters, Forster was constrained to commit the kind of "faking" of which he accuses George Meredith in *Aspects of the Novel*; he injures psychological consistency in the interest of plot and theme.[10] Forster's faking is evident elsewhere. When Margaret, at the beginning, does not accompany Helen to Howards End, Tibby's hay fever seems a natural enough explanation. But when she does not rush to be with Helen after her crisis with Paul (allowing the meddling Mrs. Munt to go in her place), Tibby's worsening condition is hardly a convincing reason. At Oniton, in her cold and brisk responses to the plight of the Basts, she comes close to betraying her faith in the holiness of the heart's affections, just as later, in the lying letter she writes to lure Helen to Howards End, she seems to be committing a crime of the heart.

In the Oniton scene, Forster tries to keep Margaret's character consistent (and admirable) by showing her as conscious of her own self-betrayals. In interceding in Leonard's behalf, at Helen's behest, Margaret is "ashamed of her own diplomacy" and of giving Henry "the kind of woman that he desired" (239–40). When her pleading is successful, she understands why some women prefer influence to the rights being sought by the suffragettes, but she also knows she has used "the methods of the harem" (240). She justifies her temporizing behavior as "Love," however, as against Helen's absolute commitment to "Truth," and willing to accept an actual rather than an ideal Henry, she rests on her lover's arm, happy in the belief that he will save the Basts as he has saved Howards End. Just at this moment, like an ironical comment, Jacky appears with her drunken revelations of Henry's adulterous past (241–43). Even after this, however, Margaret "play[s] the girl," as Henry, claiming that "[w]e fellows all come to grief once in our time," makes his callow apology (257–58).

Margaret's persistence is a tribute to Forster's belief that an ideal of love exists beyond mere sexuality. Musing on Henry's affair with Jacky, Margaret finds her faith in "comradeship" stifled (251); yet comradeship—often associated with tenderness—remains an ideal in *Howards End*. Nor need we restrict the ideal by relating it to the "Uranian" philosophy of Edward Carpenter, who wrote of comradeship in a homosexual context.[11] Like Shelley in *Prometheus Unbound* (1820), Forster tried to conceive of a transexual love that, when deployed socially, would provide for the Basts of the world "hope on this side of the grave" (215). Against this standard, even Helen fails: "She could pity, or sacrifice herself, or have instincts, but had she ever loved in the noblest way, where man and woman, having lost themselves in sex, desire to lose sex itself in comradeship?" (326). More mystical than Marxist, Forster's conception appears symbolically in Margaret's thoughts of the wych-elm: "It was a comrade, bending over the house, strength and adventure in its roots, but in its utmost fingers tenderness" (215).

If Forster's positive ideal is nebulous, his negative target is clear by the end of the novel: marriage as practiced in the Edwardian period. On more than one occasion, the narrator refers to the "glass shade" (182, 269–70) that cuts married people off from the world. Recalling Shelley's "dome of many-colored glass" that, in *Adonais* (1821), "stains the white radiance of eternity," Forster's metaphor implies a moral rather than metaphysical imprisonment, and a social rather than ontological distance from the ideal. Independent as Margaret remains, she yet succumbs to "a social pressure that would have her think conjugally" (182). Of Forster as novelist, the same cannot be said. Despite the intention stated in his notebook journal to acquiesce in social conventions, he could not acquiesce, in the end, in the use of the fictional convention that, more than any other, worked to confirm the existing social structure. Thus it is, perhaps, that Margaret, even as she idealizes heterosexual love, transforms "the marriage of Evie and Mr. Cahill into a carnival of fools" (252). For Helen, the wedding is more repugnant still: "the starched servants, the yards of uneaten food, the rustle of overdressed women, motor-cars oozing grease on the gravel, rubbish from a pretentious band" (331).

Seventeen years after *Howards End*, in his treatment of plot in *Aspects*, Forster anticipated in remarkable ways contemporary suspicions of the novel's "police" role in the "plotting" of heterosexual monogamy as a social norm.[12] Why is it necessary, he asks, that novels end in conventional ways with either death or marriage? Viewing plot as "a sort of higher government official" intent on the regulation of human affairs, he imagines "plot" speaking: "Individualism is a most valuable quality. . . . Nevertheless, there are certain limits, and these limits are being overstepped."[13] "Plot" here sounds like Henry Wilcox laying down the law against Helen's spending the night at Howards End. And if we turn to that climactic sequence in the novel, we may see how much more effective it is that the moderate Margaret, rather than the radical Helen, should be the agent of Forster's critique of both sexual and social conventions.

Still in search of her rainbow bridge, Margaret has betrayed both her sister and her own standards by acceding to her husband's view that Helen's strange behavior betokens mental illness. But when Henry and Mr. Mansbridge—the doctor he has enlisted in his scheme—seek to apprehend Helen without Margaret's knowledge, Margaret, who on the trip to Oniton had leapt *out of* the car in protest against the juggernaut of patriarchal insensitivity, on this occasion jumps *into* the car for the same reason. Nor, this time, does she apologize for her action. Recognizing that "the pack" is "turning on Helen to deny her human rights," Margaret believes that all Schlegels are threatened along with Helen (301). Henry's question ("Is the truant all right?" [302]), like the crude response of the doctor to Helen's revealed pregnancy, confirms her in that sense. As the males—Henry, Mr. Mansbridge, the chauffeur, and the driver of Helen's cab—come together for the kill, Forster's meaning is clear: at such a time, "man" is no "bridge" to a better social world. "A new feeling came over her: she was fighting for women against men. She did not care about rights, but if men came into Howards End it should be over her body" (303).

In the reunion of the sisters that follows inside the house, Forster provides the novel's most eloquent connection. After initial mistrust, Helen warms to Margaret's overtures, not because of their logic but because they are made in the rooms where Miss Avery has set out the Schlegels' furniture, an action (earlier countermanded by Margaret) that magically effects a connection between the dead and the living Mrs. Wilcoxes. That Howards End should prove hospitable to the furniture from Wickham Place is fitting in more than one sense; a rural tradition opens itself to an urban culture—though not entirely: it is a nice touch that Miss Avery has not unpacked the art books.

As their furniture is warmed and given new life in the house, so Howards End is in turn revived. As for the Schlegel sisters: "[A]ll the time their salvation was lying around them—the past sanctifying the present; the present, with wild heart-throb, declaring that there would after all be a future, with laughter and the voices of children" (313). When Henry subsequently refuses to permit Helen to stay the night, Margaret's reply is the most powerful speech in the novel: "You shall see the connection if it kills you, Henry! You have had a mistress—I forgave you. My sister has a lover—you drive her from the house. . . . Stupid, hypocritical, cruel—oh contemptible!—a man who insults his wife when she's alive and cants with her memory when she's dead. A man who ruins a woman for his pleasure, and casts her off to ruin other men. And gives bad financial advice, and then says he is not responsible. These men[14] are you" (322). Reviewing her speech later, Margaret decides that it needed to be made—not only to Henry but to "thousands of men like him"—as "a protest against the inner darkness in high places that comes with a commercial age" (347). Once more Forster connects the inner and the outer, the private and the public, the sexual and the social. As a novelist, his concern was with domestic life, but in domestic life he found the blindness and the cruelty that vitiated social life, as well as the tolerance, kindness, love, and respect for personal relations that, potentially, might ennoble and improve society. It is easy—too easy—to dismiss Forster's liberal values as "the tired platitudes of a past world,"[15] just as it is possible, from a more conservative position, to resent Forster's treatment of the

Wilcoxes. But for those who share with the Schlegel sisters the desire that "public life should mirror whatever is good in the life within," temperance, tolerance, and sexual equality will remain "intelligible cries" (28), and the inner darkness of those in high places will remain contemptible.

Yet if, after paying tribute to Forster's characterization of Margaret and Helen, we ask whether Forster was fair to the Wilcoxes, the answer—Lawrence's view notwithstanding—must be no. Several manuscript draft passages that did not appear in the final text allow for a more sympathetic reading of Charles. For example, a draft version of Mrs. Munt's first view of Charles in chapter 3 (16) is favorable: "His clothes were perfect, his voice gentle, his manners self-possessed, his complexion healthy, but not plebeian. Decidedly things might have been worse."

In the final text, Henry has a potential that is never quite fulfilled. His stature is not consistently established in his speeches. Unlike Kurtz in Conrad's *Heart of Darkness* (1902), he does not rise to eloquence in defense of the (indefensible) colonization of Africa, and unlike Andrew Undershaft in Shaw's *Major Barbara* (1905), Henry is not consistently the forceful spokesman for the world of business and commerce he seems intended to be. He is at his best during the days of his courtship and engagement, when his manner—brisk rather than brusque— sometimes convinces us that such a man might indeed be attractive to an intelligent woman like Margaret. But even then, his "masterly ways" militate against tenderness, as when, without warning, he first kisses Margaret in Aunt Juley's garden in Bournemouth (192). Appropriately, Margaret is reminded of an earlier kiss in a garden—that between Helen and Paul—and the scene is not only a euphemism for the probable nature of their subsequent sexual relationship but another instance of the ineradicable brutality of the Wilcoxes in both private and public realms. It is not that Forster fails to expose his hollow men; rather, their hollowness is sometimes too visible. Particularly toward the end, Henry's character is excessively trivialized by the speeches Forster gives him. During the honeymoon, for example, Henry addresses Margaret as follows: "What a practical little woman it is!

What's it been reading?"[16] "It" has been reading theosophy, an interest of Margaret's first mentioned at the Simpson's luncheon. Though Forster's point is clear—that men's endearments objectify and diminish women—it is too crudely made, and Forster's attempt on this occasion to thematize the opposition between male practicality and female intuition fails.

If Forster is unfair to the Wilcox men, what shall we say of his treatment of Leonard Bast? Perhaps the main problem with Leonard's characterization is that he is more often an object than a subject of discourse. He appears in person in only 7 of the novel's 44 chapters, though he has a continuing offstage existence as the object of Margaret and Helen's concern, Tibby's occasional supercilious attentions, and Mr. Wilcox's social Darwinist remarks. Diffident and deferential to an extreme, Leonard is the object of Forster's sympathy as he seeks to better himself through art, literature, and music. But he is seldom granted much dignity as a subject. When Forster uses the *style indirect libre* to communicate Leonard's thoughts, he is at a much greater distance from his character's consciousness than he is with Margaret and Helen, more given to generalizations, more apt to sermonize.

This narrative distance is particularly evident in chapter 41, in which Forster describes Leonard's life from his brief sexual encounter with Helen at Oniton up until his death at Howards End. We learn of the "remorse" that has governed his life regarding both Helen and Jacky and of his new tenderness to the latter (expressed in his willingness to scrounge off his relatives so that he can provide his wife with "a few feathers and the dishes of food that suited her" [334]). Leonard's milieu—his sisters Blanche and Laura, his brother the lay reader—is described in the sketchiest of ways. His deterioration into a professional beggar, his shiftlessness, the servility with which he goes about finding Margaret's whereabouts, are all doubtless credible as a picture of a man demoralized by economic deprivation and an ill-suited wife. But they assort somewhat awkwardly with the remorse and need to expiate his sin that Forster presents as moral qualities in Leonard. As for the journey to Howards End that takes him past the six trees in the churchyard, which grew, as legend has it, from the atheist's grave, this is more successful as theme than as characterization: Leonard, whose family came to the city from the country, is returning home; as he passes "the villas of business men" he goes back in time from an urban and secular society to a rural world in which superstitions still flourish. His individuality dwindles in the service of narrative commentary: "Here men had been up since dawn. Their hours were ruled, not by a London office, but by the movements of the crops and the sun" (338). Returning to his yeoman status (but only in death), he passes a symbol: a motor car. "In it was another type whom Nature favours—the Imperial" (338).

That Forster had trouble with Leonard's characterization is evident from a long unused manuscript draft for chapter 41. Along with references to Tristan and Isolde, which Forster wisely dropped, this draft contains material that he might have done well to retain: for example, he wrote of a period of employment that Leonard had as "a book-keeper in a commercial hotel at Exeter." During this time, Leonard "had enough to eat, saved a little, kept Jacky comfortable, and was again touched by the world's exasperating beauty." He regains his interests in culture and in nature, and thinks of visiting a cathedral by moonlight, of walking on Dartmoor, of taking a trip in a boat "with those fisherman fellows." These details, together with his speculations on the sea and its symbolic connections with death, give Leonard at least the glimmerings of an independent life that is largely absent from the finished novel.

Forster's attempts to characterize Leonard through his speech also pose problems, as the next chapter will show. But of all the aspects of the novel, speech is the one in which Forster most excels. Indeed, I would argue that Forster's ability to reproduce speech places him high among English novelists. His conversations and dialogues are superbly effective in capturing the social and political atmosphere of the time. As mimesis, however, they are not always reducible to didactic ends, and this will be matter for discussion in the chapter that follows.

"Here we are — Good morning Miss Schlegel."

Helen replied "Good morning, Mr Wilcox."

Helen had such a nice letter from the queer cross boy — do you remember him — a big mans task he has, but the back of his head was young.

"I have had letters too? — I want to talk them over with you: "the magic triangle of sex was broken now ... has given him the word. Thanks to you, Henry, he's cleaning out of the Porphyrion."

"Not a bad business about the Porphyrion" he said absently, as he took his own letter out of his pocket.

"Not a bad —", she exclaimed, dropping his hand. "Surely on Chelsea Embankment —"

"Here's our listers — Good morning, Mrs Munt. fine rhododendrons. — Good morning, Frau Liesecke; we manage to grow flowers in England, don't we?"

"Not a bad business?"

"No — My letter; about Howards End. Bryce has been ordered abroad, and wants to sublet it. I am not sure that I shall give him permission. In my opinion, subletting is a mistake. If he can find me another tenant, whom I consider suitable, I may cancel the agreement — Morning, Schlegel —; don't you think

Manuscript page of *Howards End*

8

Conversations

He never noticed the lights and shades that exist in the grayest conversation, the finger-posts, the milestones, the collisions, the illimitable views. (195)

Forster invites his readers to be less obtuse than Mr. Wilcox. Forster's conversations, like those of Jane Austen, his mentor, are at once realistic and thematic—he loads every rift with ore. As shown in the manuscript page reproduction opening this chapter, in many scenes he strives to achieve the condition of drama, minimizing his reliance on "he said" and "she replied," and identifying his characters by their idiolects (individual speech patterns). Like a playwright, he stylizes rather than simply reproduces speech and dialogue, recalling but also heightening the conversations of the people he had heard in the colleges of Cambridge, the drawing rooms of Weybridge and Bloomsbury, and the European pensions in which he stayed on his travels. Outside an Austen novel (or an Oscar Wilde play), dialogue is seldom so witty or economical as in the following exchange between Margaret, here upholding the value of work, and her 19-year-old brother, Tibby, down from Oxford, and a cynic in the Lytton Strachey line. Margaret speaks first:

> "I want activity without civilization. How paradoxical! Yet I expect that is what we shall find in heaven."
> "And I," said Tibby, "want civilization without activity, which, I expect, is what we shall find in the other place."

"You needn't go as far as the other place, Tibbikins, if you want that. You can find it at Oxford." (116)

Following such an exchange, we should not be surprised that the man the Schlegels have employed to clean the knives and boots shares a name with the famous grande dame in *The Importance of Being Earnest* (1895); like the Cambridge in-joke about Oxford dilettantism, "Bracknell" alerts us to Forster's indebtedness to Wilde's play. Forster was something of a frustrated playwright, and among his unpublished plays in the archives at King's College one may discover the evidence of considerable dramatic talent. The conversations in his farcical *The Deceased Wife's Husband* are often very funny, in a sub-Shavian kind of way; in his more serious, and covertly homosexual, *The Heart of Bosnia*, the conversations often achieve an impressive and dignified irony.

Forster had a keen ear not only for idiolects but for sociolects; in characterizing the intellectual Schlegels and the practical Wilcoxes, he uses syntax, diction, idiom, and speech rhythms to excellent effect. He is less successful when he ventures beyond his middle-class milieu, resorting to stage cockney, for example, in his representations of Jacky's speech. Even so, it is at the level of dialogue that the novel's concern with connection reveals many of its most interesting facets.

Before examining the problems of linguistic connection between the Schlegels, the Basts, and the Wilcoxes, I should give some attention to Forster's ventriloquial skills. As we have seen, he distinguishes between the idiomatic French of Margaret and the execrable French of Henry, and as always, he has an excellent ear for the English of Italians, as he shows in the brief exchange between Margaret and the Italian chauffeur in chapter 25. Germans, however, are a particular object of imitation in *Howards End*; he displays perfect pitch in capturing the not-quite-idiomatic, though grammatically correct, English of the Schlegels' German cousins. Here is Fräulein Mosebach trying to defuse Helen's "delicate situation" now that the Wilcoxes have arrived as their neighbors in Wickham Place: "Hark! . . . I hear Bruno entering the hall" (60). Here is the same woman (now Frau Architect Liesecke) engaging with Aunt Juley in what becomes a comic version of Anglo-

German trade rivalry; the issue is whether water, as at Pool Harbour, needs to move in order to be healthy, as Mrs. Munt insists it must:

> "And your English lakes—Vindermere, Grasmere—are they then unhealthy?"
>
> "No, Frau Liesecke; but that is because they are fresh water, and different. Salt water ought to have tides, and go up and down a great deal, or else it smells. Look, for instance, at an aquarium."
>
> "An aquarium! Oh, *Meesis* Munt, you mean to tell me that fresh aquariums stink less than salt? Why, when Victor, my brother-in-law, collected many tadpoles—"
>
> "You are not to say 'stink'," interrupted Helen; "at least you may say it, but you must pretend you are being funny while you say it."
>
> "Then 'smell.' And the mud of your Pool down there—does it not smell, or may I say 'stink, ha ha'?" (175–76)

Forster's mimicry is equally satirical in his representations of varieties of English speech. In chapter 33, when Margaret visits Howards End, she encounters Miss Avery's social-climbing niece, who peppers her conversation with references to her servants and is mortified when the farmyard chickens rush up to her for food. But it is her formal diction and syntax that expose her middle-class aspirations: "Mrs. Wilcox, could I prevail upon you to accept a piece of cake?" (280). Miss Avery, relic of a time before class consciousness expressed itself in speech, bluntly rejects her niece when, hat on head, the latter escorts Margaret to Howards End: "Madge, go away. This is no moment for your hat." Madge, "gathering up her elegancies," retires defeated (282–83).

Miss Avery is a touchstone in Forster's exposure of Dolly Wilcox also. Dolly is not pretentious, merely dim and without a mind of her own. During the postfuneral discussions at Howards End, she infuriates her husband and father-in-law with her fatuous interruptions (chapter 11), and responding to Margaret's account of her meeting with Miss Avery, she asks: "Did you take her for a spook?" Forster adds that, for Dolly, " 'spooks' and 'going to church' summarized the unseen" (211). Dolly has several functions in the novel, including that of revealing information at inopportune times, but in characterizing her as an empty-headed wife and mother, Forster uses speech to dramatize her superficiality. Like Jane Austen's silly characters—Anne Steele, for example, in *Sense and Sensibility*—Dolly is given to colloquialisms and dreadful puns—as when she responds to the information that Tom Howard was the last of the male Howards with "I say! Howards End—Howard's Ended!" (213); elsewhere, she relies on tautologies, clichés and stereotypes to make sense of life. Thus, Miss Avery is "dotty," in Dolly's view, because she never got married (276).

Evie is Forster's unsympathetic portrait of the masculine, athletic woman whose conversation is limited to cricket averages, bridge scores, and dogs. When Evie becomes engaged to Percy Cahill, Forster wickedly represents the banality of their *égoisme à deux* during the luncheon at Simpson's in the Strand. Their conversation, the narrator tells us, is of the "No, I didn't; yes, you did" type. Though it may be fascinating to those engaged in it, such conversation "neither desires nor deserves the attention of others" (159). As a setting, Simpson's, "with its well-calculated tributes to the solidity of our past" (160), is a restaurant for plutocrats and imperialists. Margaret, as she converses with Mr. Wilcox, overhears the jarring talk of others: " 'Right you are! I'll cable out to Uganda this evening,' came from the table behind. 'Their Emperor wants war; well, let him have it,' was the opinion of a clergyman" (160).

In the speeches of "Henry's set"—Sir James Bidder, the Fussells, the Cahills, Mrs. Warrington Wilcox—on the way to Evie's wedding, Forster exposes the brittle attitudes of other imperialists, who mouth platitudes about tariff reform while misidentifying the Oxford colleges. As in *A Passage to India* later, Forster allows his Anglo-Indian characters to condemn themselves out of their own mouths: Lady Edser declares Evie's wedding to have been "quite like a Durbar" (232), and Colonel Fussell, blithely unconcerned over the cat killed by their car, pontificates sentimentally, "Ah, a dog's a companion! . . . A dog'll remember you" (224). As usual, Forster represents critically both the brisk efficiency and the insensitivity of public-school types through their utterances. Here, for example, is Charles taking stock of the codicil to his mother's will: "A note in my mother's handwriting, in an envelope addressed to my father, sealed. Inside: 'I should like Miss Schlegel (Margaret) to have Howards End.' No date, no signature. Forwarded through the matron of that nursing home. Now, the question is—" (101). One is not surprised that Siegfried Sassoon (in May 1918) should have admired Forster's "power of reproducing conversations." As he contemplated writing "a novel dealing with the bad side of the officer class in wartime," Sassoon believed that the "superior, self-possessed voices" of the staff officers, properly reproduced, would in themselves constitute "an indictment against militarism."[1]

Forster's satire, however, is not limited to imperialists and businessmen; intellectuals, too, come under his scrutiny as, with an unerring ear for false straining after effect, he records the talk of the guests at "the little luncheon party" held in Mrs. Wilcox's honor (chapter 9). Mrs. Wilcox is of a different generation from the young intellectuals who engage in "clever talk" (77), less to communicate with her than to impress her (and each other) with their avant-garde tastes. As they discuss whether there is such a thing as "Stettinicity" (reminding present-day readers, perhaps, of the more precious of the devotees of Roland Barthes), Mrs. Wilcox (to hazard another analogy) comes on like Barbara Bush at Wellesley. While Margaret and her friends discuss the comparative merits of the painters Böcklin and Leader, Mrs. Wilcox thinks it is "wise to leave action and discussion to men" (80).

Forster's satire in this chapter is directed mainly at intellectualism. At the end of the luncheon, Margaret admits to Mrs. Wilcox that she and her friends "lead the lives of gibbering monkeys" (81), and earlier she sees that the unintellectual Mrs. Wilcox has "a personality that transcended their own and dwarfed their activities" (79). These recognitions anticipate Margaret's postmarital movement "from words to things" (274). Partly the consequence of her duties as a wife, Margaret's withdrawal from participation in the latest movements causes concern among her Chelsea friends but is presented as positive: "It was doubtless a pity not to keep up with Wedekind or John, but some closing of the gates is inevitable after thirty, if the mind itself is to become a creative power" (274). Moreover, Forster repeatedly implies that Mrs. Wilcox's non- or even preverbal world is superior to that of the verbal Schlegels. Mrs. Wilcox seems intuitively to know of Helen's affair with Paul, for example, just as—we are invited to assume—she knows that Margaret will in the end receive Howards End. Her spiritual depth is repeatedly suggested by the sea imagery that attaches to her, whereas Margaret's rationality places her—figuratively speaking—on land. After Mrs. Wilcox's death, Margaret thinks of her as a "wave" that "had strewn at her feet fragments torn from the unknown" (106). After Leonard's death she thinks: "At such moments the soul retires within, to float upon the bosom of a deeper stream, and has communion with the dead. . . . She [the soul] alters her focus until trivial things are blurred" (347). The last sentence takes us back to Mrs. Wilcox at the end of chapter 9 ("with each word she spoke, the outlines of known things grew dim" [81]); there is no doubt that Forster invites us to view Mrs. Wilcox—and her house—as a figure for spiritual meanings that are beyond the power of logic and language to express. Margaret, the impatient Londoner, at first mistrusts "the periods of quiet that are essential to true growth" (82). Later, at Howards End, an unexpected love of England is awakened in her, "connecting on this side with the joys of the flesh, on that with the inconceivable." She understands that this love comes "through" the house and Miss Avery (and therefore, by implication, "through" Mrs. Wilcox), but "her mind trembled towards a conclusion which only the unwise have put into words" (213–14). The unseen in *Howards End* is also the unsaid, but unlike the "boum" of the Marabar caves in *A Passage to India*, the translinguistic world here seems benificent and regenerative. Similarly, Mrs. Wilcox is described as tired and sad before her death, but she never becomes nihilistic like Mrs. Moore in *Passage*. It is not hard to see why good critics have described the movement toward vision in *Howards End* as a movement away from language and conversation.[2]

Yet, valued as she is for her spiritual qualities, Mrs. Wilcox hardly comes off well at the luncheon. She is a foil to the febrile posturings of Margaret's friends, but it is in the nature of her gift that she is unable to defend or define her views verbally. After Margaret gives a spirited account of the willingness of Germans to discuss vital questions with "humility," Mrs. Wilcox replies that she is too old for that, adding, "We never discuss anything at Howards End" (80). As the luncheon party episode shows, conversation may fail utterly to become dialogue, and particular discourses may remain as far apart as the forms of life they express and circumscribe. As Margaret insists, however, discussion keeps a house alive, and discussion in the form of talk between individuals and groups would seem to be essential for the perpetuation of the liberal and humane values Forster admired. That Forster had a lifelong faith in the value of people talking to one another is worth recalling, at any rate, if only to counter the idea that in *Howards End* he wholly forsook rational discussion for a counter-Enlightenment mysticism.

From 1928 onward, Forster had a close connection with the British Broadcasting Corporation (BBC), and in 1931 he began giving a fortnightly series of broadcast book reviews. In February 1932 he and his policeman friend Bob Buckingham broadcast a dialogue in a series called "Conversations in the Train," Buckingham's character taking the part of the police and Forster's that of the public. The dialogue sought to remove misconceptions about the police while upholding the right of the public to grumble and complain. It is of less interest for the conclusions it reached, however, than for its effort to make connections, through the important medium of radio, between individuals from different social and educational backgrounds. It is possible that the BBC conversation was Forster's way of fulfilling in life the kind of encounter that comes to nothing in *Howards End*: "Perhaps the keenest happiness [Leonard] had ever known was during a railway journey to Cambridge, where a decent-mannered undergraduate had spoken to him. They had got into conversation, and gradually Leonard flung reticence aside. . . . The undergraduate, supposing they could start a friendship, asked him to 'coffee after hall,' which he accepted, but afterwards grew shy, and took care not to stir from the commercial hotel where he lodged" (128). In Forster's own life, conversations in trains across class boundaries were not taboo, as a 3 December 1905 entry in his notebook journal shows. There, Forster recounts a conversation he had with a ganger's wife who boarded a train with a child at March in Cambridgeshire. The man in the next compartment had refused to open the door. "I thought people always opened the door, even if it was a poor person," the woman commented. Forster was willing not only "to open the door" but to listen sympathetically to the woman's story of a life of hardship and poverty.

With Forster's positive attitude toward conversation in mind, we may now ask to what affirmative uses he puts speech and dialogue in *Howards End*. The question obviously takes us to the Schlegels rather than the Wilcoxes. The speech of the Wilcoxes is seldom free from Forster's parodic stylization and—when it rises above sport and politics—expresses in reductive ways the theories of Adam Smith, Malthus, and Bentham. Their direct, self-confident voices, as Forster impersonates them, drown out the "goblin footfalls" that both Helen and the narrator hear. The Wilcoxes have no desire for dialogue with the lower classes, preferring to consolidate their status and maintain their separation by bullying porters and chivying chauffeurs. It is entirely appropriate that Paul Wilcox, at the end of the novel, should respond to his father's news that Margaret will leave Howards End "to her nephew, down in the field," with a coarse comment about "piccaninnies" (357).

Wilcoxes and Basts come into contact on only three occasions in the novel. The first is in chapter 16, on the afternoon of the tea at Wickham Place, when a possible rapprochement between Leonard and the Schlegel sisters is destroyed by the entry of Mr. Wilcox and Evie, attended by her puppies Ahab and Jezebel. The second, in chapter 26, is the fiasco at the wedding feast at Oniton, where it is revealed that the only conversation likely to occur between a man like Henry and a woman like Jacky is "conversation" in its eighteenth-century sense of sexual intercourse. The third occasion is the final encounter at Howards End, in chapter 41, between Charles Wilcox ("I now thrash him within an inch of his life" [339]) and Leonard that results in Leonard's death.

On Margaret and Helen, then, the onus of establishing social connections through conversation falls. Like Jane Austen's heroines, they are politically powerless but possess the power of words. Though their speech also is stylized, they represent Forster's values: a faith in personal relations, moderation, and tolerance, a love of art and literature, and a concern for social reform. And though they are occasionally open to the charge of being too intellectual, Forster distinguishes their speech from that of their more superficial and sophisticated "Chelsea" friends. The question, however, is not only whether the Schlegels' conversations signify their intelligence, vitality, and wit (consistently they do), but whether these qualities can have beneficial social and political effects on the lives of the poor (the Basts), whom they wish to help, or on the behavior of those in positions of power (the Wilcoxes), whom Margaret at any rate wishes to humanize. Can they, through their conversations, be the bridge connecting poverty and power?

Forster addresses at the end of chapter 5 the question of the effectivity of conversation: the sisters, following their first brief encounter with Leonard Bast, try to understand why they failed to put him at ease. Various reasons exist. Socioeconomic difference is a major factor; if Leonard at Queen's Hall suspects Helen of stealing his umbrella, Aunt Juley at Wickham Place is worried about the security of the Schlegels' apostle spoons, their "little Ricketts picture" (44), and the majolica plate.[3] Then again, given "Auntie Tibby's" personality, Wickham Place is hardly welcoming to "real" men (44). And yet, more important perhaps than either economic or sexual factors is the cultural gap opened by the Schlegels' conversation.

When Margaret first talks to Leonard Bast after the concert at the Queen's Hall, her speeches "fluttered away from the young man like birds" (41). Conversant with the artistic impressionism of Monet and the musical impressionism of Debussy, critical of Wagner for his "muddling of the arts," able to pronounce *Tannhäuser* correctly, Margaret receives coldly Leonard's stilted responses to her long, fluent speeches on their walk to Wickham Place. Forster gives us Leonard's thoughts: "Oh, to acquire culture! Oh, to pronounce foreign names correctly! Oh, to be well-informed, discoursing at ease on every subject that a lady started! But it would take one years. With an hour at lunch and a few shattered hours in the evening, how was it possible to catch up with leisured women who had been reading steadily from childhood?" (41).

Evidently, a major part of Leonard's problem in connecting with the Schlegels is the sheer articulateness of Margaret's middle-class speech; quite apart from *what* she says, *how* she says it intimidates him. It is not merely her effortless cultural range of reference and the confidence of her verdicts, but the accent and intonations of her voice and the way she "twist[s] her face about so" (57) that terrify Leonard. Helen, supposedly, is different and would have responded to Leonard's stilted "When my work permits, I attend the gallery for the Royal Opera" (39) with enthusiastic and friendly agreement. Helen is indeed warmer than her sister, as Forster charmingly shows in the scene at Howards End in which she greets the child with the milk, asks him his name, and tells him her own (313). But Helen can be quite as intimidating as Margaret, and the semiotics of her speech and gestures also bewilder and demoralize Leonard. When told that she has taken Leonard's umbrella, she replies: "I do nothing but steal umbrellas. I am so very sorry! Do come in and choose one. Is yours a hooky or a nobbly? Mine's a nobbly—at least, I *think* it is." A moment later, she continues: "Don't you talk, Meg! You stole an old gentleman's silk top-hat. Yes, she did, Aunt Juley. It is a positive fact. She thought it was a muff. Oh heavens! I've knocked the In and Out card down. . . . do tell the maids to hurry tea up. What about this umbrella? . . . No, it's all gone along the seams. It's an appalling umbrella. It must be mine" (41–43). But, of course, the umbrella is Leonard's, and Leonard, listening to Helen's hyperboles—as distinctive a sign of class difference as the In and Out cards and the maids—has nothing to say in reply. Murmuring a few words of thanks, he flees. Conversation here fails, as it does later when Leonard comes to Wickham Place for tea and, asked by an "over-expressive" Helen whether he wants "the big cake or the little deadlies," replies with a "waggish" cockney wit she quite fails to appreciate (144).

It may be worth recalling at this point an actual occasion on which another failure of communication occurred, again over a meal, between persons of very different social—and language—back-grounds. I refer to the famous breakfast at King's College, in 1915, at which Bertrand Russell introduced D. H. Lawrence to Maynard Keynes. The meeting with Keynes made Lawrence "mad with misery and hostility and rage." Various reasons, including his opposition to homosexuality and to "significant form," have been adduced for Lawrence's dislike of Bloomsbury, though not of Forster. But what Lawrence stressed—as in this reference to another Bloomsbury en-counter, a weekend spent with David Garnett and Francis Birrell—is his dislike of their conversation: "To hear these young people talk really fills me with black fury; they talk endlessly, but endlessly—and never, never a good thing said. . . . There is never . . . any outgoing of feeling and no reverence."[4]

The relevance of Lawrence's remarks is not that they describe the talk of the Schlegel sisters. Plainly, Forster intended Margaret and Helen to say good things and to have feeling and concern for Leonard and his predicament. Moreover, as we have seen, Forster had problems with precious talk; his own voice and conversational tone, if one cares to test the matter by listening to tapes in the National Sound Archives in London, are unlikely to have annoyed Lawrence during the brief period of their close acquaintance in early 1915.[5] Lawrence, in any case, approved of Howards End. And yet, all this conceded, do we not occasionally hear in Forster's imitations of the sisters' speech, and see in his descriptions of their facial gestures and physical movements, mannerisms militating against the very connection with Leonard that they seek?

Where Lawrence's response to Bloomsbury may also have rele-vance is in its oppositional character. Unlike Leonard, who comes as a supplicant to the seat of culture in Wickham Place, Lawrence met Russell and Keynes as an equal, with a voice of his own, opinions to defend, and neither apologies for his background nor concessions as to its not being a culture. What is most troubling about Leonard is his servility. Forster means us to sympathize with Leonard as the victim of an oppressive and exclusionary system. But even as he holds the world of culture as responsible as the world of business for Leonard's tragedy (thus, Leonard is killed by the falling books as much as by the sword wielded by Charles), he also hangs on to culture as the necessary counterforce to the laissez-faire world of competitive capitalism. Forster blames Leonard for believing in "sudden conversion" to culture and adds, "[O]f a heritage that may expand gradually, he had no conception" (52). In certain ways, *Howards End* carries on that tradition—descending from Wordsworth, Coleridge, and Arnold—that assigns to the guardians of culture the responsibility for maintaining "cultivation" in a materialistic world. No more than Wordsworth responding negatively, in his preface to the *Lyrical Ballads* (1800), to gothic novels and "sickly German tragedies" is Forster capable of affirming popular culture. He can find nothing in Leonard's milieu worthy of approval; for him, "cockney" is a term of disparagement only, and Camelia Road is not a possible alternative culture, with resources of its own, but—as his mimesis is meant to show—a subculture of the most dismal kind. The phatic exchanges between Leonard and his fellow clerk, Mr. Dealtry, at the beginning of chapter 6, the banal conversation between Leonard and his neighbor, Mr. Cunningham, that follows, and most of all, the flat and insipid dialogue between Leonard and Jacky in the basement flat—all are intended to testify to a world that is impoverished in more than an economic sense.

Thus it is that the third factor in Leonard's death is his own constitutional weakness. Not for Forster any Leavisite sense of the values inherent in a lower-class, nondenominational heritage; when the family in the flat above sings "Hark, my soul it is the Lord," the tune gives Leonard "the hump" (56). Nor for Forster any Eliotic (or Waughian) appreciation of the English music hall; when Jacky sings: "On the shelf, / On the shelf, / Boys, boys, I'm on the shelf" (54), we are not encouraged to recall Marie Lloyd.[6] Jacky's bursts of song are, instead, the sign of a woman incapable of sustaining "the art of conversation" (54) and yet another measure of her incompatibility with Leonard, whose performance of Grieg on the piano sends Jacky to bed.

I am not denying that culturally impoverished cockney households existed in the 1900s or claiming that Forster limits his cultural criticism to what Matthew Arnold in chapter 3 of *Culture and Anarchy* (1869) called the "populace"; part "barbarians," part "philistines," the Wilcoxes are equally the target of Forster's critique. Or more so—Leonard at least aspires to culture and is accomplished to a degree, as a manuscript draft for chapter 5 makes clearer than the final version: in it, Leonard says he has the pianoforte score for *Tannhäuser* and enjoys playing the piece. What I am suggesting is an asymmetry in the conversational exchanges between the Schlegels and the Basts: on the Schlegels' side, the obligation to educate and enrich; on Leonard's side, the need to learn. This asymmetry is most obvious in chapter 14, when Leonard comes to Wickham Place to try to explain away Jacky's mistake. Embarrassed and evasive, he speaks at first in a wooden syntax. When he tries to express his love for nature by citing the works of George Meredith, R. L. Stevenson, and F. L. Lucas, he communicates no more successfully, for Margaret and Helen do not appreciate these literary mediations of the experience of his nocturnal walk; they want the experience itself. Only when Leonard, "with unforgettable sincerity," admits that the dawn was not "wonderful" do they respond with enthusiasm, inspiring him to talk with fluency (125).

But Forster's intentions here are not wholly successful. We are asked to accept that the Schlegel sisters and Leonard have, for a moment, connected on a ground that is neither that of "professional athletes" (124), who go about walking in a more businesslike way with maps and compasses, nor that of the literati, whose only contact with the earth is in the pages of R. L. Stevenson, or Richard Jefferies, or George Borrow. Like Leonard, Helen and Margaret are "born adventurers" (they have backpacked in the Apennines); and though Leonard even now shows signs of reverting to his bookish allusions— and decides it may be better not to risk a second interview—truer relations (to use a Forsterian formula) would seem to gleam.

But can we respond as asked to the Schlegels' critique of culture? Not only are Margaret and Helen, on the evidence of their conversations, extremely cultured women, possessed of a detailed and extensive knowledge of art, music, and literature, but their critique of Stevenson,

Borrow, and Lucas is—we may suspect—less a critique of literature than a critique of literature that is, from a Bloomsbury point of view, démodé. True, the narrator seeks to distinguish between the books in themselves and the false uses to which they are put, but the impression nevertheless remains that Leonard was getting his ideas from the wrong (Victorian) sources. Another problem, however, is that Leonard, even when divested of his false cultural aspirations, does not speak with the spontaneity he should, or Forster presumably intends (125).

Altogether gentler in attitude than his Bloomsbury colleague Keynes, Forster yet shared with that apostle of a new liberalism a belief in an intellectual (rather than a social) aristocracy, a faith in the pedagogic role of a humane and educated bourgeoisie.[7] We may see these attitudes in the tactful but educational letters he wrote to Bob and May Buckingham; they are also present in Margaret's views, expressed in a crucial speech to Henry Wilcox during their lunch at Simpson's. Henry, fascinated and bewildered by Margaret's verbal creativity, asks her if she is not speaking to him as incomprehensibly as she had recently spoken to Leonard at Wickham Place. Margaret replies:

> I don't believe in suiting my conversation to my company. One can doubtless hit upon some medium of exchange that seems to do well enough, but it's no more like the real thing than money is like food. There's no nourishment in it. You pass it to the lower classes, and they pass it back to you, and this you call "social intercourse" or "mutual endeavour," when it's mutual priggishness if it's anything. Our friends at Chelsea don't see this. They say one ought to be at all costs intelligible, and sacrifice—" (162)

Sacrifice what? Margaret's sentence is rudely curtailed by Henry, who, "thrusting his hand into her speech," provides as predicate—"[l]ower classes" (162). But if Henry's answer is obviously not what Margaret intended, her completion is open to debate. "Intellectual complexity" is one possibility; but I propose that she intended to say "cultural heritage," and that what she refuses to do is sacrifice a slowly acquired and richly complex cultural identity in order to communicate with (in

Henry's phrase) the "lower classes." Such would be a lowering of conversation, a leaching of culture, a rapprochement with the masses at the cost of values and standards that she—and her forebears—had developed and defended. Like Margaret (and unlike her presumably more socialistic Chelsea friends), Forster does not want to sacrifice cultural literacy to achieve a spurious social harmony. Rather than a system of exchange ("money"), he wants conversation to be "food," to be sustenance. Ironically, however, Margaret makes her case at Simpson's ("no more Old English than the works of Kipling" [160]), where Henry's chosen menu of saddle of mutton, cider, and Stilton cheese is as much a medium of exchange as sustenance—each of the items being coded as "English." Thus, when Henry asks Margaret to admit that "there are rich and poor," Margaret wonders whether he understands her better than she understands herself. If conversation, like culture itself, is merely an epiphenomenon of money—independent thoughts being the product of an independent income—then conversation, like culture, will perpetuate the divisions it seeks to heal.

That Forster was partly aware of this problem of conversation is evident in chapter 5, when he sets the Schlegels' conversation *sub specie aeternitatis*: "[t]he conversation drifted away and away . . . and the great flats opposite were sown with lighted windows. . . . Beyond them the thoroughfare roared gently—a tide that could never be quiet, while in the east, invisible behind the smokes of Wapping, the moon was rising" (46). And as the chapter ends with the image of "an ill-fed boy" who exists beneath the "superstructures of wealth and art" (46), we are left with the impression that satisfactory relations between the propertied middle class and those aspiring to that status are bedeviled not only by economic factors but by the failure of conversation to be an effective means of connection.

It is unnecessary, however, precisely to determine Forster's attitude toward the social role of conversation. In discussing speech and dialogue, we are dealing with mimesis, precisely that feature of literature in which, as Socrates forces Adeimantus to admit in book 3 of Plato's *Republic*, authorial control is endangered in and by the very act of impersonating a character's speech. What is suspect as discourse

to the philosopher seeking an unimpassioned and objective truth, however, may be of interest to the reader who values fiction over science,
or philosophy for its ability to give voice to a variety of social positions.
As I have argued, we should not expect, in Aristotelian fashion, that
the multiple fictional positions impersonated by Forster reduce to a
single Forsterian voice, expressing general truths about human nature.
Forster's achievement may be more justly appreciated (in Bakhtin's
terms) for its dialogical rather than its monological character; and
while in the heteroglossia of *Howards End* certain voices are preferred
to others, no single voice—not even Margaret's—prevails in the end.
Moreover, when we move from the mimetic to the diegetic—to the
voice of the narrator—we find no stability of commentary or unity of
vision there. Whether the narrator is a single authoritative voice, and
whether, indeed, he is always a "he," are among the questions to be
discussed in the next chapter.

9

The Narrator

You may laugh at him, you who have slept nights out on the veldt,
with your rifle beside you and all the atmosphere of adventure pat.[1]
And you also may laugh who think adventures silly. But do not be
surprised if Leonard is shy whenever he meets you. (129)

Forster's admonitory address to not one but two sorts of reader separates him from the high aesthetic modernism that descended from
Flaubert and James. Their heirs were Conrad, Ford, the early Joyce,
Woolf—authors who refined themselves out of existence while assidu-
ously protecting the aesthetic autonomy of their novels. Skeptical in
Aspects of the Novel of those who were "zealous for the novel's
eminence," Forster was equally skeptical of the modernist emphasis
on point of view, as it had recently been formulated in Percy Lubbock's
neo-Jamesian *The Craft of Fiction* (1921). For Forster, point of view
was not "the fundamental device of novel-writing," as James and
Lubbock claimed; though he had had no sustained intention in *Howards End* of destroying his readers' willing suspension of disbelief,
neither had he found it necessary, in pursuit of realism or form, to
maintain a Jamesian, limited third-person point of view.[2] Margaret
Schlegel is, in James's terms, a center of consciousness, but compared
with, say, Lambert Strether in James's *The Ambassadors* (1903), she
is not—as the epigraph sufficiently shows—the consistent filter of her
author's views.

This is not to say that Forster was unable to dramatize his narrative and themes. As illustrated in the previous chapter, Forster possessed a dramatist's ability with dialogue, and his narrator is often little more than a device to set a scene or, in minimal ways, to link the speeches of characters (see the manuscript page reproduced at the opening of chapter 8). Regularly, too, he used the *style indirect libre* to embody in third-person discourse the thoughts of a character. On the other hand, as I argued in chapter 4, Forster also used the *style indirect libre* to stitch threads of commentary into the narrative "text." Just as often, Forster ignored the Jamesian imperative to integrate ideas into speech or dialogue or the represented thoughts of a privileged character. When Aunt Juley travels by train from King's Cross to Hilton, for example, she is only the occasion, not the filter, of the narrator's social criticism: "At times the Great North Road accompanied her . . . awakening, after a nap of a hundred years, to such life as is conferred by the stench of motor cars, and to such culture as is implied by the advertisements of anti-bilious pills" (14–15).

Often, for purposes of characterization, Forster makes use of the omniscient narrator. For example, having dramatized Margaret's character through her speech in an early scene, Forster adds: "Away she hurried, not beautiful, not supremely brilliant, but filled with something that took the place of both qualities—something best described as a profound vivacity, a continual and sincere response to all that she encountered in her path through life" (10). Less sympathetically, he sums up Dolly: "She was a rubbishy little creature, and she knew it" (95). Indeed, chapter 11, in which this comment appears—the chapter that describes the Wilcoxes at Howards End following the funeral of Mrs. Wilcox—is a good example of Forster's pragmatic attitude toward point of view. At the beginning we are given an aerial view of the funeral as Forster momentarily inhabits the thoughts of a woodcutter, who looks down on the ceremonies from a tree; we are also granted access to the thoughts of the woodcutter's mother and the gravediggers, who share fond memories of Mrs. Wilcox and a dislike of the surviving Wilcoxes. In such a scene Forster's technique is closer to Tolstoy's than to James's.

Later in the same chapter, Forster combines a dramatic representation of the brisk, functional, and insensitive speeches of the Wilcoxes with, instead of psychological analysis, old-fashioned descriptions of their physiognomies. Here, for example, is Mr. Wilcox: "His face was not as square as his son's, and indeed the chin, though firm enough in outline, retreated a little, and the lips, ambiguous, were curtained by a moustache. But there was no external hint of weakness. The eyes . . . were the eyes of one who could not be driven. The forehead . . . [a]t times . . . had the effect of a blank wall. He had dwelt behind it, intact and happy, for fifty years" (94).

Forster's shifts between omniscient and limited points of view, and between dramatic and third-person representations, do not in themselves diminish his power "to bounce the reader into accepting what he says."[3] But on several occasions Forster endangers his mimesis by "laying bare" (in Russian formalist terminology) the narrator's function in the novel. Not infrequently, the narrator intrudes in the story as an *I* addressing or assuming a reader. For example, when Mr. Wilcox, to Margaret's amusement, reveals "huge drawbacks" in his Ducie Street house—drawbacks earlier concealed from Margaret when she was a possible tenant—the narrator imagines Mr. Wilcox's annoyed response to anyone who might impugn his motives, adding: "So does my grocer stigmatize me when I complain of the quality of his sultanas, and he answers in one breath that they are the best sultanas, and how can I expect the best sultanas at that price?" (190).

Again, during the scene in which the bereaved Wilcoxes justify their suppression of Mrs. Wilcox's legacy to Margaret, the commentator steps forward: "Ought the Wilcoxes to have offered their home to Margaret? I think not. The appeal was too flimsy. It was not legal; it had been written in illness, and under the spell of a sudden friendship; it was contrary to the dead woman's intentions in the past, contrary to her very nature, so far as that nature was understood by them" (102–3).

When Forster's narrator "steps forward" in these ways, he seems most at variance with the integrative and realistic aims of fictional modernism. Conrad provides an obvious contrast of technique in *Heart of Darkness*, in which he dramatizes his narrator, Marlow, by making him an actor in the events that he both narrates and evaluates. Conrad also dramatizes Marlow's audience by creating the narrative frame in which Marlow's fellow sailors aboard the cruising yawl *Nellie* listen to his nightmare tale of the moral deterioration of Kurtz in Africa, while they wait for the tide to turn in the Thames estuary.[4] Though the director, the lawyer, the accountant, and the anonymous figure who writes down Marlow's tale are in effect a surrogate readership against whose responses readers may measure their own, Conrad does not, as Forster does, cross the boundary between art and life, or point to the artificiality of his representation by confusing those inside the book's covers with those outside.

Yet Forster's intrusive technique, far from seeming crude and old-fashioned, may well commend itself to contemporary readers. Fictional realism is not here concealing an ideological agenda under the guise of truth; rather, with a deliberate frankness, Forster's narrator announces his presence and acknowledges his views and prejudices. Point of view is as much political as rhetorical. In technique Forster is closer to Trollope than James—to the Trollope who in *Barchester Towers* (1857) tells the reader that he himself could never bear to shake hands with the oily Mr. Slope, the evangelical chaplain in the novel.

The narrator's prejudices may be of a trivial sort. As the (male) editor of Helen's letters in the first chapter, he omits details of the clothes worn by Helen, Mrs. Wilcox, and Evie (4), details we are to assume Helen included. If clothes are outside his competence (or beneath his interest), so too, on the occasion of the encounter between Mrs. Munt and Charles Wilcox, is the motorcar ("Young Wilcox was pouring in petrol, starting his engine, and performing other actions with which this story has no concern" [17]). Of more serious import is the narrator's bald statement at the beginning of chapter 6: "We are not concerned with the very poor." Though this—the most notorious of the narrator's intrusions—may be interpreted as Forster's staking out of the area of his representational expertise, the statement's shock value tends to exceed all attempts at palliation. The narrator explains that Leonard, "at the extreme verge of gentility," is not one of the very poor: "They are unthinkable, and only to be approached by the statistician or the poet. This story deals with gentlefolk, or with those who are obliged to pretend they are gentlefolk" (47). "Unthinkable" must surely mean "beyond the power of Forster to conceive." But does it not also carry a meaning close to "unspeakable"? If so, the word can still be understood ironically, as expressing a brittle class attitude distinct from Forster's own; but he—or his narrator—is treading dangerous ground.

Such intrusions separate *Howards End* from the goals and techniques of fictional modernism, but their disruptive power may be downplayed or ignored. We may still construct for the narrator a coherent, humanistic identity—by aligning him, for example, with the viewpoints of Margaret, the novel's most privileged character. Indeed, Margaret's claim to being the normative consciousness in the novel is aided, on one occasion, by an act of extraordinary empathy on the narrator's part. At Oniton, Margaret has decided to go ahead with her marriage to Henry in spite of Jacky's revelations. Why? In his answer, Forster trangresses the rules of the *style indirect libre* by shifting from the third-person singular to the first-person plural: "Pity was at the bottom of her actions all through this crisis. Pity, if one may generalize, is at the bottom of woman. When men like us, it is for our better qualities, and however tender their liking we dare not be unworthy of it, or they will quietly let us go. But unworthiness stimulates woman. It brings out her deeper nature, for good or for evil" (254). From *her* to *us*, from *one* to *we*, the passage effects a momentary identification between (male) narrator and (female) character before retreating from first person to third and reestablishing the distinction of levels and sexes. As Elizabeth Langland has argued, the passage is evidence of Forster's sympathy for the female point of view.[5] It does not, however, entitle us to assume a consistently female narrative consciousness.

That the narrator gives voice to views that, on the basis of our knowledge of his essays and broadcasts we may describe as "Forsterian," seems a more likely proposition. Yet if we heed Wayne Booth's arguments, we will not make the mistake of confusing the dramatized narrator with the biological author.[6] True, the narrator of *Howards End* is reliable, rather than unreliable in the manner of the narrator in Ford Madox Ford's *The Good Soldier* (1915). Reading Dowell's first-person narration in the latter novel, readers quickly come to distrust his perspective and to seek behind it for a perspective that Ford intends. Unlike Ford, Forster endorses his narrator's commentaries, which—or so it may be argued—closely resemble his political views.

One way to qualify this persuasive argument is to provide a selective list of the narrator's roles and to ask whether they constitute a consistent ideological position. Among other things, the narrator is: a social commentator deploring the urbanization of England and the emergence of a "civilization of luggage"; an ecological Cassandra warning of the effects of pollution; a lover of the countryside; a Burkean defender of heritage against the inroads of economic individualism; a compassionate woman; a defender of the imagination; a critic of businessmen and the utilitarian calculus; a judicial arbitrator of probate law; a mythopoeist of England; a writer of a county guide; an essayist or sermonizer on such topics as the role of culture, the meaning of death, and the psychology of remorse; a lover of music (especially Beethoven) and the rural spring (especially in Hertfordshire); an enemy of imperialism, social Darwinism, and the motorcar; an English chauvinist; a critic of English insularity; a critic of cosmopolitans; a Cambridge man skeptical of the Oxford mentality; and an opponent of public schools, the masculine ethic, and a society in which heterosexual monogamy is enforced as the human norm.

Can we subsume the above roles (and the contradictions they occasionally imply) into the various expressions of a composite Forsterian persona, rather as Leonard Bast finds the bewilderingly voluble Margaret and Helen to be "a composite Indian god whose waving arms and contradictory speeches were the product of a single mind" (147)? We have to concede that the above roles are by and large congruent with a liberal-progressive, Cambridge-educated, middleclass Weltanschauung. But the heterogeneity of the narrator can hardly be ignored. He—or, as on the remarkable occasion noted above, she—occupies a number of subject positions and speaks in a variety of voices that are not easily reducible to a single ideology.

Moreover, the narrator addresses a variety of posited readers, who exist at a greater or lesser distance from the narrator's various concerns and sympathies. These readers include: men who are afraid of emotion; friends of the earth; insular moralists; lovers of Beethoven; rationalists who deny an "unseen" reality; imperialists who are insensitive to the needs of the poor and the exploited; those who depreciate adventure; and those who, by virtue of money and heritage, have culture in their bones. Addressing such readers, the narrator can be cordial, inviting assent to his humanistic propositions, or defensive, aware of objections from readers who do not share his values.

The variety of readers dramatized in *Howards End* should, in itself, warn interpreters not to assume an ideal or transcendental reader of Forster's text. It is not a case here—as it may be in interpreting *Heart of Darkness* and *The Good Soldier*—of seeking to recover a set of values that exist behind the perspective of the narrator and are the product of the author's strategic rhetorical intentions. (Whether any novel succeeds in achieving a perspective that is univocal, coherent, and recoverable by all competent readers is, in any case, a debatable question.) Instead, Forster's technique in *Howards End* invites us to view both narrator and reader as plural entities. The narrator's plurality is limited, to some extent, by Forster's upbringing and background, by his period and its available discourses, and by a certain tone or voice—variously cozy, congenial, arch, wise—that several generations of readers have recognized as Forsterian. The reader's plurality is obviously not limited in these ways, and the greater the historical distance between *Howards End* and its readership the greater will be the plurality of the reader. Even in 1910, however, some of Forster's attempts to position himself in relation to different viewpoints must have seemed odd. How many of his readers, for example, had slept all night on the veldt with a rifle beside them? And how did grocers respond to his construction of their defense of overpriced sultanas?

Occasional failures of effect aside, the narrative discourse of the novel is, in complex and successful ways, dialogical. Itself plural, it assumes the existence of a plurality of readers, who are to be addressed, debated, inveigled on a variety of propositions. Ought the Wilcoxes to have offered Howards End to Margaret? It is a good question, one that invites us to take time out from the story and argue a case that has both legal and human dimensions, a case that is not closed, even after the narrator's judicious commentary. If readers object to the position presented in this or other instances, or to the narrator's construction of the reader as an addressee, they are free to demur (as many have done, and do, in the form of more or less indignant marginal comments). But readers may also agree with the narrator's arguments (or with some of them), take lessons from his essays and sermons, reflect on his wise proposals, and give enthusiastic—or qualified—assent to his positions. An important consequence of Forster's intrusive narrator is likely to be a wary, even resistant reader, who is neither lost in the fictional illusion nor intent on the recovery of universally valid meanings but instead enters into a series of dialogues and debates with the propositions of the text.

What active reading might entail I shall shortly suggest, but a brief divagation on Forster's use of personal pronouns is here appropriate. As we have seen, Forster's narrator may appear as an *I*; but the narrator may also appear as a *one*, a *we*, and even a *you and I*. Both *one* and *we* are, of course, grammatically convenient pronouns; they permit the writer to avoid a too insistent egoism whole also claiming for his or her propositions a consensual validity (in this way I use both pronouns repeatedly in this study). As pronouns, however, both *one* and *we* are subject to suspicion. *One*, for example, often makes a presumptive claim to a certain social and educational status; it becomes a class marker and may be used, intentionally or unintentionally, as a signal of superiority, a gesture of separation. Hilda Rowbotham in D. H. Lawrence's short story "The Christening" (1914) provides a good example. The eldest daughter of an upwardly mobile miner, Hilda is a schoolteacher who has received a college education. As the story opens, however, she is embarrassed by her younger sister's having given birth to a baby out of wedlock. Though Hilda does not know it, the father is the baker's man at Berryman's, a fact that partly explains the surliness with which the shopkeeper tells her that he is out of macaroons. Hilda's speech in reply, however, provides another explanation of his dislike: "Then I can't have any, Mr. Berryman. Now I do feel disappointed. I like those macaroons, you know, and it's not often I treat myself. One gets so tired of trying to spoil oneself, don't you think? It's less profitable even than trying to spoil somebody else."[7] Like Lawrence, Forster was aware that *one* could be a pretentious pronoun; in Leonard's reply to Jacky's nagging, for example, he captures the falsity of Leonard's speech (imperfectly imitative as it is of the speech of the Schlegels): "It really is too bad when a fellow isn't trusted. It makes one feel so wild, when I've pretended to the people here that you're my wife" (55). Forster's sympathy for the "very poor" (despite his narrator's disclaimer) was unstinting, and his satiric exposure of middle-class pretensions and proprieties (the behavior of Mrs. Herriton in *Where Angels Fear to Tread*, of the Pembrokes in *The Longest Journey*, of the Wilcoxes in *Howards End*) puts him in the company of Jane Austen and Samuel Butler as a satirist of bourgeois falsity. And yet he had never been—as Lawrence had—one of the poor.

In this recognition, Forster's narrative uses of *one* and *we* hardly seek or achieve grammatical neutrality; rather, the pronouns imply a middle-class perspective, even as they invite readers' agreement. Such invitations are obviously not without risk; much will depend on the tone of the invitation, on the tact with which it is transmitted, and on the nature of the opinion or topic in question. Much will depend, too, upon the background and outlook of particular readers: will a reader assent to the narrator's assumption of a shared agreement on particular questions, or find the narrator's preemptive construction of his or her response to be morally and politically objectionable?

In the nature of the argument, I cannot speak of the responses of "particular" readers, but perhaps I can ask for an assent to the proposition that the narrator's intrusions in *Howards End* make different claims on "our" willingness to approve. When, for example, the narrator enthuses over the London railway stations in a way that is surely typical of Forster, the use of *we* is not objectionable: "They are our gates to the glorious and the unknown. Through them we pass out into adventure and sunshine, to them, alas! we return. In Paddington

all Cornwall is latent and the remoter west; down the inclines of
Liverpool Street lie fenlands and the illimitable Broads; Scotland is
through the pylons of Euston; Wessex behind the poised chaos of
Waterloo" (12). The narrator's comments here emerge from—and can
be viewed as an extension of—the "strong feelings" that Margaret has
"about the various railway termini" (12). But as the narrator goes on,
the point of view first expands to include the feelings of Italians who,
exiled in Berlin, "call the Anhalt Bahnhof the Stazione d'Italia, because
by it they must return to their homes" (12), then contracts to express
the tendency of all but the "chilly Londoner" to extend to the London
stations "the emotions of fear and love" (12), and finally contracts
further as the narrator returns to Margaret, whose viewpoint, however, is now separable from that of the narrator: "To Margaret—I
hope that it will not set the reader against her—the station of King's
Cross had always suggested infinity. Its very situation—withdrawn a
little behind the facile splendours of St. Pancras—implied a comment
on the materialism of life. . . . If you think this ridiculous, remember
that it is not Margaret who is telling you about it; and let me hasten
to add that they were in plenty of time for the train" (12). Forster's
management of grammatical persons is deft, as *she* (Margaret), *we*
(the narrator and those readers assumed to be in agreement about the
romance of railway stations), *they* (nostalgic Italians in exile), *he* (a
typical Londoner), *I* (the narrator playing a protective role toward his
character), and *you* (readers, prosperous capitalists perhaps, who are
skeptical of Margaret's romantic viewpoint) coexist dialogically in the
same stretch of prose. It is not that the narrator's sympathies are
unclear; like Margaret, he is in love with railway stations and sees
them as "fit portals for some eternal adventure" inexpressible in "the
ordinary language of prosperity" (12). But in the dialogism of the
passage he allows for difference of opinion and a variety of viewpoints.
Instead of being absorbed in the drama of Mrs. Munt's trip to rescue
Helen, for a moment we can consider where we—variously—stand,
not only on the question of railway stations as a possibly universal
focus of national sentiments, but on the potential and permissible
meanings of architecture.

It is surely a different matter when the narrator invites us, in chapter 6, to acquiesce in his negative appraisal of Jacky, on the occasion of Leonard's accidental smashing of the glass frame holding her photograph: "It represented a young lady called Jacky, and had been taken at the time when young ladies called Jacky were often photographed with their mouths open. Teeth of dazzling whiteness extended along either of Jacky's jaws, and positively weighed her head sideways, so large were they and so numerous. Take my word for it, that smile was simply stunning, and it is only you and I who will be fastidious, and complain that true joy begins in the eyes" (50). "You and I"? Speaking for myself, I cannot accept the narrator's invitation to "fastidious" fellowship here or assent to the commonality of experience assumed in the narrator's following proposal that Jacky's flowery hat "resembled those punnets, covered with flannel, which *we* sowed with mustard and cress in our childhood" (53) (emphasis added). Furthermore, recalling the narrator's lack of interest in the dresses worn by Helen and the Wilcox women in chapter 1, I wonder why the narrator spends so much time detailing Jacky's "awesome" appearance here (52). Not that it is unlikely that Jacky, in the words of an unused manuscript draft, "looked a perfect sight," or that this "massive woman of thirty-three" was "descending quicker than most women into the colourless years" (54, 53). What is objectionable is the invitation to join a censure that is not only external and sarcastic but assumes that sartorial taste is a natural possession of the middle class.

Forster's failure of tact and sympathy is never again so prominent in *Howards End*; although the narrator's appraisals of Leonard raise questions, they differ from his views of Jacky. When Leonard arrives at Wickham Place for the second time, the reader encounters (or, more accurately, readers encounter) "a young man, colourless, toneless, who had already the mournful eyes above a drooping moustache that are so common in London, and that haunt some streets of the city like accusing presences. One guessed him as the third generation, grandson to the shepherd or ploughboy whom civilization had sucked into the town; as one of the thousands who have lost the life of the body and failed to reach the life of the spirit" (120). What is the status of "one guessed" in this citation? Leonard's arrival is clearly the occasion for a brief essay in sociological analysis (of the kind Masterman had recently conducted in *The Condition of England*) and for an expression of doubt as to the humanizing effects of culture on those who had left the countryside for London. But the guessing here at least partly emerges from the three Schlegel siblings, who hurry downstairs in a spirit of curiosity to see this alien specimen. *One* is also the transition to Margaret's consciousness, which may once again reflect Forster's, though we cannot be sure. When we read that Margaret "knew this type very well—the vague aspirations, the mental dishonesty, the familiarity with the outsides of books" (120), we need not assume that Forster also is claiming to "know" Leonard Bast in the same condescending and essentializing way as Margaret does.

Forster's use of *one* at the beginning of chapter 19 is less easily transferable to the consciousness of a character. Since the passage it introduces has been the subject of a good deal of critical dialogue, it is of particular relevance to the present discussion. "If one wanted to show a foreigner England," the narrator begins, "perhaps the wisest course would be to take him to the final section of the Purbeck Hills, and stand him on their summit, a few miles to the east of Corfe" (174). In the long paragraph that follows, the narrator describes the actual view from this station, as well as the view that can be imagined to the north—of "Salisbury Plain itself, and beyond the Plain to all the glorious downs of Central England" (174). Although *one* here is vaguely attached in the second paragraph to Mrs. Munt, who brings the German cousins to be impressed by the view (they prove recalcitrant), neither she nor Helen, who accompanies her, is the source of the extraordinary enthusiasm that irradiates Forster's prose, quoted in part in what follows:

> Seen from the west, the [Isle of] Wight is beautiful beyond all laws of beauty. It is as if a fragment of England floated forward to greet the foreigner—chalk of our chalk, turf of our turf, epitome of what will follow. And behind the fragment lie Southampton, hostess to the nations, and Portsmouth, a latent fire, and all around it, with double and treble collision of tides, swirls the sea. How many villages appear in this view! How many castles! How many churches, vanquished or triumphant! How many ships, railways and roads!

What incredible variety of men working beneath that lucent sky to what final end! The reason fails, like a wave on the Swanage beach; the imagination swells, spreads and deepens, until it becomes geographic and encircles England. (175)

Not all readers have been impressed. F. R. Leavis found Forster's " 'poetic' communication . . . at this level of poeticality" to be vague, sentimental, even immature. K. W. Gransden described it as a "patriotic purple patch"—an example of the failure of Forster's "inner ear," as opposed to the successes of his "outer ear." For Peter Widdowson, the England presented here, like the England of the Georgian poets, is an idealized vision that excludes from view the realities of rural as well as urban life.[8] Such critiques have force and cogency.

Kenneth Graham, however, defends Forster's passage, seeing it as another attempt to mediate the impersonal and unseen realities elsewhere represented by the ghostly Mrs. Wilcox or by Beethoven's music in the Queen's Hall. The passage, in Graham's view, resembles the vision that the whole novel is trying to encircle through imaginative means. As the landscape described by the narrator also becomes the stage of the confrontation between Margaret and Helen over Margaret's engagement to Henry, it expresses Helen's sense of division as well as Margaret's search for connection. At the end of the chapter, however, when Forster returns to test the landscape anew in another charged and poetic description, he is able, like Beethoven, to compose in a major key and, though not definitively or finally (for questions still remain), to put the "goblins" to flight. Graham's formalist reading is eloquent and helpful; but it is a formalist reading, intent on forging, as much perhaps as finding, internal connections.[9]

In a less formalist view, the descriptions in chapter 19 are good examples of ekphrasis. Such descriptive passages, essentially detachable fragments, are a common feature in literature and typically carry thematic and political meanings. Gransden is partly right in comparing Forster's prose to a travel advertisement.[10] Like the passages in William Camden's *Britannia* (1586) and Michael Drayton's *Poly-Olbion* (1613, 1622)—which attempted in prose and verse to provide a *specu-*

lum Britanniae—or like those in Defoe's Whig paean in prose, *A Tour through the Whole Island of Great Britain* (1724–26), Forster's descriptions are a form of scenic patriotism.[11] In the *Tour*, Defoe actually anticipates Forster in taking foreigners to a prospect that epitomizes England; Defoe's prospect, viewed from Bushey Heath, has the town of St. Albans on the right with interspersed corn fields, villages, and hedgerows and, in the distance, a view of the west end of London with Westminster Abbey and Parliament-House. Defoe's foreigners, unlike Forster's, are impressed by the combination of city and country, nature and art, in the prosperous scene before them. One of them says to the other, in "a kind of wonder," that "England was not like other country's, but it was all a planted garden."[12]

Forster's view differs from Defoe's in its negative disposition toward social and commercial progress. True, he includes Southampton and Portsmouth in the prospect, but he—or rather, his narrator—notes critically the "trail" of London commerce and the stock exchange, evident in the "ignoble coast" of Bournemouth. "But the cliffs of Freshwater it shall never touch," the narrator adds defiantly (if not quite convincingly), "and the island will guard the Island's purity till the end of time" (174–75). The description also includes a general reference to an "incredible variety of men working"; but it scarcely represents industrial (as opposed to commercial and imperialistic) England. Clearly, the narrator's imagination did not take him as far north of Salisbury Plain as Birmingham, not to mention Liverpool or Leeds. And for those persuaded by Martin Wiener's argument that nostalgia for the countryside has been a major reason for Britain's industrial decline, the limitation in Forster's imagined "view" will be a cause for concern.[13]

Two considerations may mitigate an ideological critique of this kind. In the first place, Forster connects the ekphrasis of the initial paragraph to the emotional confrontation of the sisters on the Dorset downs. Both sisters appeal to the landscape in this episode. Unassuaged by Margaret's remarks, Helen can respond to her sister's engagement to Henry only with the cry of "panic and emptiness"; she "break[s] away and wander[s] distractedly upwards, stretching her hands towards the view and crying." Margaret, following her sister "through the wind that gathers at sundown on the northern slopes of the hills," is suddenly seized with stupidity, and "the immense landscape was blurred" (180). As Graham shows, the effect of this scene is to qualify, complicate, perhaps even counteract the imaginative vision of the first paragraph. Margaret insists that "if Wilcoxes hadn't worked and died in England for thousands of years, you and I couldn't sit here without having our throats cut"; as she speaks, however, she waves her hand at the landscape, which, the narrator tells us, "confirmed anything" (183). Secondly, when Forster's narrator returns to the landscape at the end of the chapter, his chauvinism may be even more Shakespearean (with obvious echoes of Gaunt's speech in *Richard II*), but the description is made up of questions, inviting readers to enter the dialogue:

> England was alive, throbbing through all her estuaries. . . . What did it mean? For what end are her fair complexities, her changes of soil, her sinuous coast? Does she belong to those who have moulded her and made her feared by other lands, or to those who have added nothing to her power, but have somehow seen her, seen the whole island at once, lying as a jewel in a silver sea, sailing as a ship of souls, with all the brave world's fleet accompanying her towards eternity? (183)

Is England to belong to the Wilcoxes or the Schlegels? to the practical imperialists or the imaginative idealists? to the doers or the thinkers? Is a marriage between these positions possible? Can such a marriage avert the horrors Helen apprehends? At the end of chapter 19, it is clear that Forster has used the Dorset landscape as a screen to project questions rather than a facile chauvinism. In a manuscript draft, Forster added to the "brave world's fleet" the specification, "ship of Germany, ship of France." Did he delete the phrase because it introduced a historical threat into his ideal vision of a future brotherhood of nations? In the years leading up to *Howards End*, Admiral John Fisher had laid down the Dreadnought class of battleships to combat the growth of the German fleet, and within four years of the novel's publication, in April 1914, the dead in Thomas Hardy's "Channel Firing" were awakened—not far from Nine Barrow Down—by "gunnery practice out at sea." As God says in the poem, all nations are "striving strong to make / Red war yet redder"; the poem ends with a haunting vision of England:

> Again the guns disturbed the hour,
> Roaring their readiness to avenge,
> As far inland as Stourton Tower,
> And Camelot, and starlit Stonehenge.[14]

Forster's vision of England in chapter 19 lacks Hardy's tragic sense of history, but it is more troubled and complex, too, than the sentimental (and mildly teutonophobic) vision of Rupert Brooke in "The Old Vicarage, Grantchester" (1912).

This is not to deny, however, that Forster could use landscape, like Brooke, to promote a quiet rural image of England. Hertfordshire —not Brooke's Cambridgeshire—is his scenic norm. Hertfordshire, the narrator tells us in the language of a county guide, "is England at its quietest, with little emphasis of river and hill" (206); and in the description in chapter 33 of "the untouched country" near Howards End the narrator gives us a far less complex use of landscape than in chapter 19: "Having no urgent destiny, it strolled downhill or up as it wished, taking no trouble about the gradients, nor about the view. . . . The great estates that throttle the south of Hertfordshire were less obtrusive here, and the appearance of the land was neither aristocratic nor suburban. To define it was difficult, but Margaret knew what it was not: it was not snobbish. . . . 'Left to itself,' was Margaret's opinion, 'this county would vote Liberal' " (279–80). In comparable ways Henry James, in *English Hours* (1905), read "Tory" meanings into the Warwickshire countryside;[15] and we may feel such equations are forced or facile. As Philip Gardner has argued, however, we need not dismiss Forster's countryside as "a pastoral vehicle for romantic wish-fulfilment, a kind of celestial omnibus."[16] Believing that England, unlike Greece, lacked a great mythology, that "the native imagination" had failed "to vivify one fraction of a summer field, or give names to half a dozen stars," Forster seems to have attempted in *Howards End*, not to be the great poet who would give voice to a mythic England, but to be one of "the thousand little poets whose voices shall pass into our common talk" (279).[17] In this role, however, he is related, intertextually, to a long line of English poets, including Chaucer, Shakespeare, Milton, Keats, and Arnold, who, delighting in the English flora and the procession of the seasons, preceded Forster in "vivifying" the English countryside they loved. In a citation like the following from *Howards End*, one may hear some of their voices and, without difficulty, turn the passage into four lines of verse: "Spring had come, clad in no classical garb, yet fairer than all springs; fairer even than she who walks through the myrtles of Tuscany with the graces before her and the zephyr behind" (281).

Far different from such poetry are the narrator's descriptions of London in *Howards End*. Like William Cobbett (and many others) before him, Forster looked on London as "an infernal wen," a city of flux and stink, monstrous in its tentacular urban extensions; like the speaker in *The Waste Land* (1922) who, viewing the crowds flowing over London bridge, "had not thought death had undone so many," he registered and deplored the sterility of modern city life.[18] "Month by month," the narrator states at the beginning of chapter 13, "the roads smelt more strongly of petrol, and were more difficult to cross, and human beings heard each other speak with greater difficulty, breathed less of the air, and saw less of the sky. Nature withdrew: the leaves were falling by midsummer; the sun shone through dirt" (112).

The narrator's sentiments here supposedly describe London during the two-year interval in the novel's action, as the Schlegels pursue their life of culture and leisure. But it is clear that the first two paragraphs of the chapter are an inserted critique of urban existence that are only in a pro forma sense integral to the narrative. When the narrator states that "one visualizes [London] as a tract of quivering grey, intelligent without purpose, and excitable without love" (112), we may or may not assent, but we are (variously) likely to engage his critique of London life—vitiated, as the narrator sees it, by pollution, mobility, anomie, and irreverence for architectural heritage. Recognizing that "to speak against London is no longer fashionable," the narrator reveals that he expects disagreement and demurral. "Of Pan and the elemental forces," he goes on, with a nod to Forster's own fictional fantasies such as "The Story of a Panic" (1904), "the public has heard a little too much," adding that "those who care for the earth . . . may wait long ere the pendulum swings back to her again" (112). We may feel, in our own period of acid rain, escaping fluorocarbon gases, and ozone depletion, that if the pendulum has not swing back now, it had better soon. To enlist Forster in a green cause would doubtless be opportunistic, however, for his antiurban attitudes, like his criticism of the motor car, are without scientific basis and carry not a little sentimental freight. To say, as the narrator says, that "London is religion's opportunity" and that it would "be tolerable if a man of our own sort—not anyone pompous or tearful—were caring for us up in the sky" (113) is hardly a template for ecological reform.

Forster's achievement as a social critic is not, however, to have proposed solutions to social problems but to have put significant topics on the table for his readers to discuss and debate. His narrator in this context is similar to the hostess who moderates the speeches at the informal discussion club in chapter 15, and his readers are similar to the discussants. The comparison may seem far-fetched if we think of the novel as a mass-produced commodity intended for the private consumption of isolated readers. In classrooms and in informal reading groups, however, the comparison holds, and the discussion at Margaret's club is a plausible enactment of what might well still happen at such meetings. The question is, how should a hypothetical millionaire dispose of his money at his death? And the answers are various. He should found an art gallery, provide a free library, pay for tennis courts. He should give his money to his eldest son. He should help poor individuals by paying for foreign holidays or providing rent subsidies or supplementing their Territorial Army pay or assigning them a "twin star." He should give them food but no clothes, or clothes but no food. And so the discussion proceeds. We need not doubt that Margaret's proposal—that he leave as many poor individuals as possible £300 per annum—is the proposal closest to Forster's heart (in his own life he was extraordinarily generous to his less well-off friends, providing many with gifts, some with pensions, and in the Buckinghams' instance, helping them buy their Coventry home). But it is the discussion that is important, and not the viewpoint that ultimately prevails. As paternalist, liberal, and socialist solutions to the problem of poverty are canvassed, Margaret's proposal (to give cash to individuals) carries Forster's approval. She is aware of the danger of charity becoming a means of social control, of money being given in restrictive ways so as to convert poverty into a middle-class image. Margaret's awareness may not seem equally enlightened to all readers, however, and her piecemeal solution to poverty might well be exceptionable to, for example, socialist readers unwilling to accept her argument that socialists "think in terms of commodities instead of cash," while treating welfare recipients like "babies" (133).

When in chapter 17 (to return to the topic of London), the narrator takes up his antiurban sentiments again ("The feudal ownership of land did bring dignity, whereas the modern ownership of movables is reducing us again to a nomadic horde. We are reverting to the civilization of luggage" [156]), we may not agree, but our various evaluations of the narrator's views may not, by now, be much affected by the very visible stitching of the topic into the narrative fabric ("It was absurd, if you came to think of it; Helen and Tibby came to think of it; Margaret was too busy with the house-agents" [156]). In similar ways the narrator stitches other topics and issues into the novel's cloth, and concerning one of these—the role and significance of death—I shall have something to say in the next, and final, chapter. In concluding these remarks on the narrator, however, I hope it is clear why Forster was right not to pursue the modernist aim of authorial impersonality. Had he done so, we should have lost a pungent and variously provocative presence, as well as frequent opportunities for interaction with the text.

10

Only Connect . . .

The teeth are almost grown over now, and no one comes to the tree.
(74)

Elegies for a past rural world coexist in Forster with dread forebodings of the future under a technological civilization. In a notebook journal entry for 27 January 1908, Forster, reacting to the news of a recent aeroplane flight, wrote:

It's coming quickly, and if I live to be old I shall see the sky as pestilential as the roads. It really *is* a new civilisation. I have been born at the end of the age of peace and can't expect to feel anything but despair. Science, instead of freeing man . . . is enslaving him to machines. Nationality will go, but the brotherhood of man will not come. . . . God what a prospect! The little houses that I am used to will be swept away, the fields will reek of petrol, and the airships will shatter the stars. . . . [S]uch a soul as mine will be crushed out.

This is the despairing Forster who, when he fails to find the present sustained by the past, looks to an apocalyptic future for an answer and, in stories like "The Machine Stops" (1908), writes against H. G. Wells's optimistic faith in technology. In the same journal entry he sees, as one alternative, "that the machine should destroy life, stop itself, and we begin again—perhaps no trees, perhaps not even water." In a locked journal entry of 19 February 1909, he wrote of "grinding out my novel into a contrast between money & death—the latter is truly an ally of the personal against the mechanical." By showing how Forster filters this theme into *Howards End*, I shall summarize the approach of this study and the findings of the previous chapters.

Helen is Forster's main spokesperson for death as the ally of the personal and the foe as well as the peer of love. When a dispirited Leonard, at Oniton, proposes that money is the fundamental reality, Helen responds that death is the measure of money and the "imperial" enemy of the imperialists. Death and money, she insists, are the "eternal foes," not death and life. "Never mind what lies behind Death, Mr. Bast, but be sure that the poet and the musician and the tramp will be happier in it than the man who has never learnt to say 'I am I'" (249). Her paradox—that "Death destroys a man; the idea of Death saves him" (250)—is partly a reprise of the old topos of "death the leveller." Despite Trilling's denial of eschatology in Forster, he is conducting an eschatological argument here, though not in an orthodox Christian sense.[1] Whether or not there is an afterlife, Forster is arguing, unless we live in the awareness of death our lives will be meaningless. The Wilcoxes, who neither take personal responsibility for their lives nor live in the knowledge of death, are thus the "hollow men" in *Howards End*, resembling the accountant in *Heart of Darkness*.

Forster takes some care to attach his meditations on death to Helen. On her visit to Howards End, Margaret, witnessing the solitary house, thinks of how Helen would "revel in such a notion! Charles dead, all people dead, nothing alive but houses and gardens" (209). But the theme of death does not "belong" to Helen; it is the narrator who, on the occasion of Mrs. Wilcox's exemplary death, provides a little sermon ("It is thus . . . that we ought to die" [107]) and who, as Mrs. Munt (apparently) lies on her deathbed, denies that "we" can generalize about the deaths of those we love (288). Moreover, it is the narrator who, as Leonard makes his fatal way to Howards End, repeats exactly Helen's paradox about the saving idea of death (339). The migratory nature of Foster's theme is most obvious, however, when the narrator, expressing Charles Wilcox's sense of regret in the third person, repeats the very words of Helen's Nietzschean explanation of the Wilcox character: "he had a vague regret . . . a wish (though he did not express it thus) that he had been taught to say 'I' in his youth" (344).

That Nietzsche is Forster's source is made explicit in chapter 27, where Helen explains the deficiency of the Wilcoxes, as follows: "There's a nightmare of a theory that says a special race is being born which will rule the rest of us in the future just because it lacks the little thing that says 'I.'" When Leonard admits, "I never got on to Nietzsche . . . [b]ut I always understood that those supermen were rather what you may call egoists," Helen replies: "No superman ever said 'I want,' because 'I want' must lead to the question 'Who am I?' and so to Pity and to Justice. He only says 'want'" (245). Needless to say, Helen's view of the *Übermensch* is prejudicial. In a work like *Beyond Good and Evil* (1886) Nietzsche examined profoundly the concept of 'I' as well as the values of pity and justice; but Nietzsche's transvaluations of these categories would have been repugnant (if not, indeed, incomprehensible) to Forster whose belief in the virtues of moral individualism and social philanthropy came to him from liberal thinkers like John Stuart Mill and his own forebears in the Clapham Sect.[2]

As my allusions to Wells, Conrad, a conventional topos, and Nietzsche indicate, however, Forster's ideas and beliefs are not really "his," except as he expresses them through his characters and commentaries, and by way of agreement or disagreement with the already expressed thoughts of other thinkers. We in turn, as I have argued in the previous chapter, may (variously) enter this intertextual field. For me, Forster-Helen's appeal to the idea of death as salvation is somewhat cold comfort (and is received as such by Leonard), and too close to the doctrine of "unequal providence" that Parson Primrose preaches for its consolatory value to the prisoners in Oliver Goldsmith's *The Vicar of Wakefield* (1766).

Forster, while often finding motivations for his ideas and themes in character (and thus composing a novel in James's sense, or a work in Barthes's sense), does not always do so. More than any other aspect, the "migration" of themes from one fictional part to another—from one character's speech to another charactor's thoughts, for example, or from a mimetic conversation here to a diegetic commentary there—testifies to the textual nature of *Howards End*. This is not a radical proposal; when Oliver Stallybrass, in his analysis of Forster's manuscript deletions and changes, writes that "Forster's desire to make some general point often preceded any sure sense of the place in the narrative where it could most naturally be introduced," he was already recognizing, in my terms, the textuality of *Howards End*.[3] Nor, as I hope I have shown, does such a recognition preclude a reader's enjoyment of Forster's fictional craftsmanship: the skill with which he incorporates a knowledge of German history or of Beethoven's music into the narrative; the subtlety of his onomastics (isn't it a secret joke that Helen's German suitor should be named Herr Förstmeister, the first and last syllables forming Forster's own name?); the ease with which he quickens narrative tempo not only to effect dramatic climaxes but to conceal didactic intentions; the thematic harnessing of games, gardens, and garages in a critique of the plutocracy; the excellence of his conversations ("Never has an intellectual atmosphere been better transferred to paper" was the opinion of the *Daily Telegraph* critic);[4] his critical representation of behavior, manners and conventions; and the keenness of his eye and ear for the distinctive signs of social difference. In all these ways, as this study has often suggested, Forster is Austen's most distinguished heir. His irony, in particular, is Austenian—as when Henry having suppressed his wife's gift of the house to Margaret, sends her a silver vinaigrette instead (163). As F. R. Leavis long ago insisted, however, though Forster is "pre-eminently a novelist of civilized personal relations, he has at the same time a radical dissatisfaction with civilization . . . that prompts references to D. H. Lawrence rather than to Jane Austen."[5] And so Lawrence too has been cited as a measure of contrast and comparison.

We now know that Forster's dissatisfaction with civilization stemmed in part from his homosexuality; but far from agreeing with those critics, who, as described in chapter 3, took the publication of *Maurice* as a reason for a negative reappraisal of Forster's oeuvre, I agree with John Colmer, when he proposes that we have in Forster "an interesting case of the creative tension between a personal ideology only belatedly raised to full consciousness and an alien social ideology enshrined in a literary form to which he was strongly attracted on stylistic grounds."[6] Pursuing this line of thought in chapter 7, I described the tension between Forster's conventional and subversive aims, but unlike Crews and Stone, the two strongest critics of *Howards End*, I do not read Forster's refusal (rather than failure) to close his novel affirmatively by way of the marriage plot as a political retreat. Speaking of *The Longest Journey*, Forster's biographer has recently written that the emphasis rests "not so much on Idealism versus Realism . . . as on the damage to our perceptions of the world fostered by monogamous love."[7] Something of this emphasis remains in *Howards End*, the main drama of which I take to be the impaired, and then restored, relationship of the sisters.

I do not claim, however, that Forster's critique of monogamous love, or his affirmation of the "inner life" of Margaret and Helen, constitutes the meaning toward which all of the novel's elements of plot, setting, character, and language dynamically tend. Against such an Aristotelian assumption, and in recognition of the splendid heterogeneity of *Howards End*—its diversity of genres and topics, its multiple discourses, its intertextual relations—I have conducted a decompositional analysis. I have not focussed on the more visionary aspects of the novel or drawn upon Forster's ideas of "prophecy" and "rhythm" as developed in chapters 7 and 8 of *Aspects of the Novel*. For me the metaphysical Forster is of less interest than the social Forster. "Infinity," in Forster's phrase, may attend Mrs. Wilcox; and like the characters in Dostoevsky, she is certainly meant to stand for more than herself.[8] When, for example, Margaret catches her dress in brambles and burrs while out walking at Oniton, we are invited to remember Mrs. Wilcox's connection with nature (226); and when the housemaid is summoned to "sweep up the long trickle of grass" that Margaret has left across the hall (260), we are reminded of Helen's letter describing Mrs. Wilcox at Howards End: "Trail, trail, went her long dress over the sopping grass" (4). Margaret is Mrs. Wilcox rediviva ("I— Mrs. Wilcox—I"). Mrs. Wilcox's significance I have seen more in historical than in spiritual ways, however, though I recognize that her negative verbal abilities are affirmed in the novel, which, in one of its trajectories, prefers intuition to logic, and the unseen to the seen.

But this is the point: *Howards End*, like all "classic" novels in Kermode's sense, says far more than any reading can encompass. All discoveries of Forster's "vision" (if I may adopt the absolute language of Helen Schlegel) exist only by the occlusion or suppression of counterfacts and contradictions. In highlighting this phenomenon of fictional interpretation, I mean to give value to Forster's novel. Unapologetic in his belief that fiction should, like Forest Reid's novels, "help," Forster—or his narrator—comes close to sermonizing, even proselityzing on behalf of liberal humanism. To interpret his novel as a secular tract for the times is hardly possible or desirable today, however; nor should we (but who is "we"?) be content to extract from the novel nuggets of wisdom that might serve as guideposts on the road of life.

Consider the following passage: "Culture does not help us make our way in a business civilization, yet it has its value and yields its return. In our attitude toward the poet and the professor we are perfectly ambivalent: we know they are useless, yet they make us humble-defiant, and the business man who declares himself a lowbrow is aggrieved if anyone agrees with him." This is not, you may have guessed, from *Howards End*; nor is it, in fact, by Forster, though with its penchant for generalizing, its prose rhythms, its syntax, diction, and—above all—its use of *we*, it sounds like Forster in one of his essays, or like Forster's narrator in one of the inserted essays in *Howards End*. The "wisdom" here is Trilling's,[9] and though he seems to be miming Forster's wisdom (that is, recovering from *Howards End* its humanistic meaning), the passage has an odd effect. In relation to what set of values is the reader being invited to join the consensus? "We" are not businessmen, it would seem; neither are "we" poets and professors, though Trilling was a professor and a novelist, and Forster a novelist who professed ideas in fiction, essays, lectures and broadcasts. *We* is hard to locate as the sign of a social or political conviction: the pronoun hovers between positions, prevented by a pervasive sense of irony from proclaiming culture (as Coleridge and Arnold did) as the answer to the ills of a business civilization, aware of culture's commodification of values, and yet in the end unwilling to give up on the idea of culture, to go "beyond culture," or to envisage one that might emerge from below.

Is the alternative to Trilling's ironically nuanced liberal-humanist interpretation the confident and powerful political critique conducted in Widdowson's study? The problem, already discussed in chapter 3, is that the latter study assumes that Forster's novel was, even in its own time, ideologically superannuated; *Howards End* has little to tell Widdowson except by way of limitation or insufficiency of vision. I agree that the limitations of Forster's vision need to be addressed rather than ignored or palliated, and his characterization of Leonard and Jacky pose difficulties indeed. Forster's awkward—deliberately awkward—relation to modernism, however, has seemed to me to provide a mode of entry to his novel which allows for a heuristic interpretation—an interpretation, that is to say, that discusses, argues with, approves, qualifies, or refutes the myriad of propositions made. Forster's distrust of plot and point of view, his refusal to refine himself out of existence or consistently to dramatize his ideas through character, speech and represented thought, his intrusive and provocative narrator (or narrator*s*)—all these aspects of his novel invite a dialogical response, not from "the reader," but from readers whose plurality is assumed and addressed in the novel itself.

It may be appropriate to end in a Forsterian way. I sometimes think I belong to the fag-end of academic humanism. In many ways the criticism it espoused was admirable, disinterested, humane, and intellectually curious. Society, it seemed, was to become better and better, chiefly through the spread of education in literature and the discussion and promotion of literary values. But though academic humanism was humane, it was imperfect, inasmuch as we were insufficiently aware of our economic position. In came our salaries (not huge, but adequate), up rose the lofty thoughts, and we did not realize that none of our students were black, few were women, or that the values we "disinterestedly" discovered in Jane Austen or E. M. Forster were at least partly determined by racial, social, and sexual presuppositions.

All that has changed in recent decades with the rise of feminist and cultural studies in the academy, and few of us would wish it otherwise. The challenge of our time, it seems to me, is to combine the new theories with the old humanism. We must be actively aware of the ideological dimensions of literature and engage these in debates in the classroom and in essays and books. But in the process we can affirm that a novel like *Howards End*, when so engaged, provides pleasure and value to the mind and—dare one say it?—the spirit.

For the past 19 years I have lived in North Florida, one of the loveliest areas in North America. During the same period, Florida has been one of the fastest-growing states in the union, with consequences, all too often, like the following (and here I break out of my Forsterian imitation to quote Bill Maxwell, a native Floridian and local columnist):

> Here it is: mile after mile of pastel-stucco houses, strip shopping centers, fast-food franchises and outcroppings of kitschy subdivisions with handles such as Foxfire, Emerald Hills and Chateau Latour. . . . And the once-beautiful coastlines that plunged the visitor onto pearly white sand dunes and into the cool waters of the Atlantic Ocean and Gulf of Mexico now seal in condo-golf resorts and empty lives. And the inexorable traffic jams and mid-day temper tantrums.

Commerce, suburbia, golf, the motorcar, anger, and emptiness, all the themes recur—the Wilcoxes have triumphed!—and even the cliffs of Freshwater (by transposition) have been touched. To read Maxwell's bitter and nostalgic column is to reencounter Forster's praise of gemeinschaft and criticism of gesellschaft; it is also to wonder just how politically regressive it is to oppose growth. Poverty and unemployment afflict many in North Florida, so that middle-class English professors find themselves facing a collision of loyalties. It is not quite the same dilemma that Forster faced in "the Challenge of Our Time" (1946); rural dwellers in North Florida are hardly likely to find a satellite town foisted upon their neighborhood by central government; the threat lies elsewhere—in the mindless, unplanned proliferation of suburbia that Maxwell describes, heralded in the name of progress and justified in terms of laissez-faire. Whether growth will help the poor and unemployed remains an open question. What seems certain is that "the precious distillation of the years" (157) will be spilled.

Describing a small Southern town, Maxwell writes: "I realized that life here was as it should be everywhere else: Experiences should be the familiar and natural outcomes of the dynamics of the place and its people. Everyone and everything should be an integral part of the community."[10] Well, this too may be debated; but Mrs. Wilcox and Miss Avery would agree, and the reason, perhaps, why Forster named his novel after a house—not a magnificent house, but a modest red-brick Hertfordshire house which had once been a farmhouse—is that he wished to pay tribute to a small community in which each member has an integral part. At the close, Howards End houses Henry and Margaret, Helen and her child by Leonard Bast. It is a diminished community, but one in which the Schlegel sisters, faithful to their father's ideals, are attempting to "rekindle the light within" (30).

Notes and References

1. Conflicts of the Edwardian Period

1. Jeremy Crump, "The Identity of English Music: The Reception of Elgar 1898–1935," in *Englishness: Politics and Culture 1880–1920*, ed. Robert Colls and Philip Dodd (London: Croom Helm, 1986), 166.

2. Michael Holroyd, *Bernard Shaw: 1898–1918: The Pursuit of Power*, vol. 2 (New York: Random House, 1989), 123.

3. C. F. G. Masterman, *The Condition of England* (London: Methuen, 1909).

4. Peter Widdowson, *E. M. Forster's "Howards End": Fiction as History* (London: Chatto & Windus/Sussex University Press, 1977), chaps. 2 and 5.

5. John Colmer, *E. M. Forster: The Personal Voice* (London: Routledge and Kegan Paul, 1975), 87.

6. Forster provides a useful account of the Clapham Sect in *Marianne Thornton* (London: Edward Arnold, 1956). Marianne Thornton, Forster's great-aunt and benefactor, was the daughter of Henry Thornton, who was the friend of the abolitionist William Wilberforce; Thornton was also the author of a respected work on paper credit and a crusading M.P. for Southwark.

7. E. M. Forster, *Goldsworthy Lowes Dickinson and Related Writings*, ed. Oliver Stallybrass, vol. 13 of *The Abinger Edition of E. M. Forster* (London: Edward Arnold, 1973), 96

8. E. M. Forster, *Two Cheers for Democracy* (New York: Harcourt Brace, 1964), 56, 57, 59.

2. E. M. Forster's Fictional Ways of Knowing

1. When the phrase appears in the novel in chapter 22, it is punctuated with an exclamation point; but as I discuss in chapter 7, Margaret's confidence on this occasion is misplaced.

2. Quoted in P. N. Furbank and F. J. H. Haskell, "E. M. Forster: The Art of Fiction I," *Paris Review* 1 (Spring 1953): 39.

3. The Critical Fortunes of *Howards End*

1. Philip Gardner, *E. M. Forster: The Critical Heritage* (London: Routledge and Kegan Paul, 1973); Frederick P. W. McDowell, *E. M. Forster: An Annotated Bibliography of Writings about Him* (De Kalb: Northern Illinois University Press, 1976); and B. J. Kirkpatrick, *A Bibliography of E. M. Forster*, 2d ed. (Oxford: Clarendon Press, 1985). McDowell has kept abreast of Forster scholarship since 1975; see his "Forster Scholarship and Criticism for the Desert Islander," in *E. M. Forster: A Human Exploration*, ed. G. K. Das and John Beer (London: Macmillan, 1979), and " 'Fresh Woods and Pastures New': Forster Criticism and Scholarship since 1975," in *E. M. Forster: Centenary Revaluations*, ed. Judith Scherer Herz and Robert K. Martin (London: Macmillan, 1982). Alan Wilde provides a thoughtful appraisal of Forster criticism and scholarship in his introduction to *Critical Essays on E. M. Forster* (Boston: G. K. Hall, 1985).

2. Gardner, *Critical Heritage*, 130, 151, 135, 156.

3. Ibid, 148, 155.

4. Ibid., 162, 136–37, 146, 149.

5. Ibid., 160.

6. Virginia Woolf, "The Novels of E. M. Forster," reprinted in *The Death of the Moth and Other Essays* (New York: Harcourt Brace, 1970), 175, 172.

7. The aesthetic disagreements between Woolf and Forster are more complicated than brief discussion can show. For a more extended treatment that argues that the art-life dichotomy has been overstressed, see Judith Scherer Herz, *The Short Narratives of E. M. Forster* (New York: St Martin's Press, 1988), 140–47.

8. Lionel Trilling, *E. M. Forster* (New York: New Directions, 1964), 13, 11–12.

9. Ibid., 19, 123, 125.

10. Noel Annan, *Leslie Stephen: His Thought and Character in Relation to His Time* (Cambridge, Mass.: Harvard University Press, 1952); Frederick C. Crews, *E. M. Forster: The Perils of Humanism* (Princeton: Princeton University Press, 1962); Wilfred Stone, *The Cave and The Mountain* (London: Oxford University Press, 1966).

11. John B. Beer, *The Achievement of E. M. Forster* (New York: Barnes and Noble, 1962), chap. 1.

12. H. A. Smith, "Forster's Humanism and the Nineteenth Century," in

Notes and References

Forster: A Collection of Critical Essays, ed. Malcolm Bradbury (Englewood Cliffs, N.J.: Prentice-Hall, 1966), 109.

13. Stone, *Cave and Mountain*, 3–5, 239.

14. John Maynard Keynes, "My Early Beliefs," reprinted in *The Bloomsbury Group*, ed. S. P. Rosenbaum (Toronto: University of Toronto Press, 1975), 52.

15. Crews, *Perils of Humanism*, 178–79.

16. Stone, *Cave and Mountain*, 237. Carolyn Heilbrun, "The Woman as Hero," *Texas Quarterly* 8 (Winter 1965): 132–41, is not cited by Stone. "Red-Bloods" and "Mollycoddles" are terms Stone borrows from Goldsworthy Lowes Dickinson, who defined them in predictable ways. For a good critique of Stone's argument, see Elizabeth Barrett, "The Advance beyond Daintiness: Voice and Myth in *Howard End*," in Herz and Martin, *Centenary Revaluations*.

17. Stone, *Cave and Mountain*, 266.

18. Wilde, *Critical Essays*, 1.

19. Samuel Hynes, "Forster's Cramp," in *Edwardian Occasions: Essays on English Writing in the Early Twentieth Century* (New York: Oxford University Press, 1972), 114–22; Cynthia Ozick, "Forster as Homosexual," *Commentary* 52 (December 1971): 81–85; Denis Altman, "The Homosexual Vision of E. M. Forster," *Cahiers d'etudes et de recherches Victoriennes et Edouardiennes* 4–5 (1977): 85–95; Joseph Epstein, "One Cheer for E. M. Forster," *Quadrant* (December 1985): 8–18. For convincing replies to such charges, and the homophobia they sometimes imply, see Wilfred Stone, "E. M. Forster's Subversive Individualism," in Herz and Martin, *Centenary Revaluations*, Claude J. Summers, "The Flesh Educating the Spirit," in his *E. M. Forster* (New York: Ungar, 1983), and Judith Scherer Herz, "From Private Self to Public Text," in her *The Short Narratives of E. M. Forster*.

20. Jane Marcus, "Liberty, Sorority, Misogyny," in *The Representation of Women in Fiction*, ed. Carolyn G. Heilbrun and Margaret R. Higonnet (Baltimore: Johns Hopkins University Press, 1983), 60–97; for a balanced rebuttal to Marcus's parti pris, see Herz, *The Short Narratives of E. M. Forster*, 145–47.

21. Patricia Stubbs, *Women and Fiction: Feminism and the Novel 1880–1920* (New York: Barnes and Noble, 1979), 219.

22. Bonnie Finkelstein, *Forster's Women: Eternal Differences* (New York: Columbia University Press, 1975), 89–116, and Elizabeth Langland, "Gesturing toward an Open Space: Gender, Form, and Language in E. M. Forster's *Howards End*," in *Out of Bounds: Male Writers and Gender(ed) Criticism*, ed. Laura Claridge and Elizabeth Langland (Amherst: University of Massachusetts Press, 1990), 252–67.

23. Widdowson, *Fiction as History*, 12.

24. Ibid., 104.

25. Peter Brooker and Peter Widdowson, "A Literature for England," in Colls and Dodd, *Englishness*.

26. Ibid., 150.

27. Crews, *Perils of Humanism*, 179–80.

28. Raymond Williams, *The Country and the City* (New York: Oxford University Press, 1973), 264–71.

29. Frank Kermode, *The Classic: Literary Images of Permanence and Change* (New York: Viking, 1975), 40–45.

4. "Work" and "Text"

1. *Russian Formalist Criticism: Four Essays*, trans. Lee T. Lemon and Marion J. Reis (Lincoln: University of Nebraska Press, 1965); Roland Barthes, *S/Z* (Paris: Editions du Seuil, 1970); Mikhail M. Bakhtin, "Discourse in the Novel," in *The Dialogic Imagination*, ed. Michael Holquist, trans. Michael Holquist and Caryl Emerson (Austin: University of Texas Press, 1981). For a consideration of the demise of the formal moment in novel criticism, see Alistair M. Duckworth, "Critical Formalities," *Georgia Review* 39 (Fall 1985): 655–61.

2. E. M. Forster, *Aspects of The Novel* (New York: Harcourt Brace, 1955), 78–79.

3. Kirkpatrick, *Bibliography*, 16. It is no doubt a small point, but whereas the Penguin edition of *Howards End* designates chapters with a simple Roman numeral, the Abinger edition prefaces the number with the word *chapter* and uses Arabic numbering. The Vintage edition used as reference text for this study divides the word *chapter* from the Arabic numeral by a thick black line. Such paratextual flourishes are unauthorized.

4. Quoted from the Penguin edition.

5. E. M. Forster, *The Manuscripts of Howards End*, correlated with Forster's final version by Oliver Stallybrass, vol. 4a of *The Abinger Edition of E. M. Forster* (London: Edward Arnold, 1973), 26.

6. Ibid., 95.

7. Charles Dickens, *Hard Times*, ed. David Craig (Baltimore: Penguin, 1969), 47.

8. Stone, *Cave and Mountain*, 102. For a more recent analysis of *Aspects* that reveals its ambivalently formalist character, see S. P. Rosenbaum, "*Aspects of the Novel* and Literary History," in Herz and Martin, *Centenary Revaluations*.

9. Forster, *Two Cheers*, 89.

10. Ibid., 82, 80.

11. Paul R. Rivenburg, "The Role of the Essayist-Commentator in *Howards End*," in Herz and Martin, *Centenary Revaluations*, 168, 174.

12. Forster, *Two Cheers*, 59–60.

13. Compare with the scene in *Emma* (chapter 6) in which the various responses of the characters to Emma's portrait of Harriet Smith suggest their characteristic weaknesses and—in Mr. Knightley's instance only—strengths.

14. Clive Bell, "Roger Fry," in *Old Friends: Personal Recollections* (London: Chatto & Windus, 1956), reprinted in Rosenbaum, *The Bloomsbury Group*.

15. Clive Bell, *Art* (1914; reprint, New York: G. P. Putnam's Sons, 1958), 30.

16. Forster, *Two Cheers*, 129, 128, 128.

17. For Forster's musical abilities, see Benjamin Britten, "Some Notes on Forster and Music," in *Aspects of E. M. Forster*, ed. Oliver Stallybrass (New York: Harcourt Brace, 1969).

18. Oliver Stallybrass, in his annotation to this scene, invites us to compare Forster's description of Beethoven's symphony with Goldsworthy Lowes Dickinson's essay in the *Independent Review* of August 1906.

5. Plot

1. Forster, *Aspects*, 23, 26; Henry James, Preface to *The Tragic Muse* (1908), reprinted in *The Art of the Novel: Critical Prefaces by Henry James*, intro. Richard P. Blackmut (New York: Charles Scribner's Sons, 1934), 84.

2. Forster, *Aspects*, 66–67, 88.

3. Ibid., 33.

4. Another difference—namely, that Helen, unlike Marianne Dashwood, becomes pregnant in consequence of her emotional nature—is of less significance. Jane Austen was constrained by social and family standards of polite discourse not to represent the pregnancy of her heroine; but Marianne's false lover Willoughby does impregnate another impressionable young woman—Eliza—whose miserable fate "substitutes" for Marianne's. Even in Forster's world, describing the pregnancy of a *respectable* woman had its perils. In the 19 September 1910 entry in his so-called locked journal, Forster wrote: "Mother is evidently deeply shocked by Howards End. The shocking part is also inartistic, and so I cannot comfort myself by a superior standpoint. . . . Yet I have never written anything less erotic" (King's College Archives).

5. Forster, *Aspects*, 29.

6. For this sociological distinction between traditional and modern

types of society, see Ferdinand Tönnies, *Gemeinschaft und Gesellschaft* (1887), discussed in Malcolm Bradbury, *The Social Context of Modern English Literature* (Oxford: Blackwell, 1971), 9–11.

7. Gardner, *Critical Heritage*, 142.

8. Mary Lago and P. N. Furbank, eds., *Selected Letters of E. M. Forster, 1879–1920*, vol. 1 (Cambridge, Mass.: Belknap Press of Harvard University Press, 1983), 136; hereafter referred to as *Letters I*.

9. Manuscript memoir on his writing life, King's College Archives.

10. For an appreciation of Forster's fictional technique based on the tea table, see Christopher Isherwood's autobiographical *Lions and Shadows* (London: Hogarth Press, 1938), 173–75.

11. *Manuscripts of "Howards End,"* Appendix A, 355.

12. Forster, *Aspects*, 96.

13. Not quite all; it has been suggested to me that he is the "hammer" and "brace" of Forster's plot structure.

14. Forster, *Aspects*, 95.

6. Setting

1. Alistair M. Duckworth, "Gardens, Houses, and the Rhetoric of Description in the English Novel," in *The Fashioning and Functioning of the British Country House*, ed. Gervase Jackson-Stops, et al. (Washington, D.C.: National Gallery of Art, 1989), 395–413.

2. Both the memoir and the sketch are among the Forster papers in the King's College Archives. The memoir was published in the Penguin edition of *Howards End* (1987) as an appendix and is hereafter referred to as Rooksnest Memoir, followed by the Penguin edition page number.

3. Forster, Rooksnest Memoir, 338.

4. Gaston Bachelard, *The Poetics of Space*, trans. Marie Jolas (New York: Orion Press, 1964), 11, 8, xxxii, 4.

5. Ibid., 6–7.

6. Quoted in P. N. Furbank, *E. M. Forster: A Life* (New York: Harcourt Brace, 1981), vol. 2, 204. The West Hackhurst memoir in the Forster Papers at the King's College Archives is not available to scholars.

7. E. M. Forster, *Marianne Thornton: 1797–1887: A Domestic Biography* (London: Edward Arnold, 1956), 269–70.

8. The Vintage edition reads "the paddock that he loved."

9. Tobias Smollett, *The Expedition of Humphry Clinker*, ed. Lewis M. Knapp (London: Oxford University Press, 1966), 325. Of several other fictional houses saved at the eleventh hour, Dumbiedykes's mansion, described

in chapter 43 of Walter Scott's *The Heart of Midlothian* (1818), is also relevant to the present discussion.

10. See, for example, his "Notes on the English Character," in *Abinger Harvest* (New York: Harcourt Brace, 1964), 4–5.

11. Quoted in Clive Aslet and Alan Powers, *The National Trust Book of the English House* (New York: Viking, 1985), 222.

12. Quoted in David Ottewill, *The Edwardian Garden* (New Haven: Yale University Press, 1989), 55.

13. Trilling, *Forster*, 119.

14. R. C. K. Ensor, *England 1870–1914* (Oxford: Clarendon Press, 1936), 414.

15. Quoted in J. G. A. Pocock's introduction to his edition of Edmund Burke, *Reflections on the Revolution in France* (Indianapolis: Hackett, 1987), xlvi.

16. Stone, *Cave and Mountain*, 263.

17. Smollett, *Humphry Clinker*, 343.

18. For good positive readings of the symbolism of the novel's ending, see John Edward Hardy, "*Howards End*: The Sacred Center," in *Man in the Modern Novel* (Seattle: University of Washington Press, 1964), and George H. Thomson, *The Fiction of E. M. Forster* (Detroit: Wayne State University Press, 1967), chap. 5.

19. Crews, *Perils of Humanism*, 122.

7. Characters

1. *Jane Austen's Letters*, ed. R. W. Chapman (London: Oxford University Press, 1964), 401.

2. Forster, *Aspects*, 47.

3. McDowell, *E. M. Forster: An Annotated Bibliography*, 660, item 1452.

4. For Lukács's discussion of the "type," see his *Studies in European Realism*, intro. Alfred Kazin (New York: Grosset & Dunlap, 1964), 6–7.

5. I take the notebook journal entry to adumbrate the intention of *Howards End* rather than *A Room with a View*. Although *Room* was not published until October 1908, it was begun in 1903; *Howards End* was started in the summer of 1908.

6. Notebook journal, 21 March 1904 entry; "minority" is a code for homosexuality, as his comments in the locked journal entry of 12 January 1912 on the "minorism" of J. A. Symons also indicate. For Forster's own account of the momentous meeting with Carpenter and Merrill, which inspired

him to write *Maurice*, see the "Terminal Note" to that novel. Not until 1916 in Egypt, however, did Forster part with, in his phrase, his "respectability" (letter to Florence Barger, 16 October 1916, *Letters I*, 243).

7. Gardner, *Critical Heritage*, 190.

8. For the suggestion that Tibby might derive from Thoby, the elder brother of Virginia Woolf, see Stone, *Cave and Mountain*, 239. More plausible is Stone's idea that Margaret and Helen derive from Thoby's sisters, Vanessa and Virginia, though Forster, in the memoir of his writing career (King's College Archives), gives the three sisters of Goldsworthy Lowes Dickinson as models. The comparison with Grant's painting is suggested by Forster's description of Tibby leaning "so far back in his chair that he extended in a horizontal line from knees to throat" (115).

9. In *Culture and Anarchy* (1869), Arnold admired Sophocles, "who saw life steadily and saw it whole"; for an excellent discussion of Forster's multiple uses of this phrase in *Howards End*, see Stone, *Cave and Mountain*, 271–73.

10. Forster, *Aspects*, 90.

11. See Edward Carpenter, *The Intermediate Sex* (1908; reprint, New York: Mitchell Kennerly, 1912), in which Carpenter argues that "it is their great genius for attachment which gives to the best Uranian types their penetrating influence and activity, and which often makes them beloved and accepted far and wide" (13).

12. See, for example, D. A. Miller, *The Novel and the Police* (Chicago: University of Chicago Press, 1988).

13. Forster, *Aspects*, 85.

14. The Vintage edition reads "These, man, are you."

15. Stubbs, *Women and Fiction*, 210.

16. Quoted from the Penguin edition (257); the Vintage edition, its editors perhaps unable to believe that Henry could be quite so condescending, reads "What's it she's reading?" (273).

8. Conversations

1. *Letters I*, 290, fn. 2.

2. See Elizabeth Langland, "Gesturing toward an Open Space" and Douglass H. Thomson, "From Words to Things: Margaret's Progress in *Howards End*," *Studies in the Novel* 15, no. 2 (1983): 122–34; for a discussion of Forster's metaphysics in relation to his use of sea imagery, see chapter 5 in John Sayre Martin, *E. M. Forster: The Endless Journey* (Cambridge: Cambridge University Press, 1976).

3. A manuscript draft has "the little Blake picture" instead of "the little

Ricketts picture." "The little Blake picture" surely refers to a copy of Blake's *Songs of Innocence* that belonged to Forster's paternal grandfather and eventually descended to him; he left this copy—"one of the finest in the world," according to Michael Halls, "The Forster Collection at King's: A Survey," *Twentieth-Century Literature* 31, nos. 2–3 (1985), 157—to King's College to mark his eightieth birthday in 1959. That Forster should originally have thought of Blake's work as the valuable property to be protected from Leonard Bast's intrusion reinforces the view that the Schlegel sisters represent Forster's values in the chapter, and that Aunt Juley perhaps speaks in the voice—and with the suspicions—of Forster's Aunt Laura, who left the Blake to him.

4. Quoted in Rosenbaum, *Bloomsbury Group*, 49, 368.

5. Forster's radio voice is that of an educated man of the upper middle class; despite an occasional drawl, it resists the temptation to be a signifier in itself. Forster seeks instead to advance an argument or conversation through a precision of phrase and an appeal to reason and logic. For available recordings of Forster's broadcasts, see Kirkpatrick, *Bibliography*, sects. F2 and F3.

6. For F. R. Leavis's defense of Lawrence and criticisms of Bloomsbury, see his "Keynes, Lawrence and Cambridge," in *The Common Pursuit* (London: Chatto and Windus, 1953), reprinted in Rosenbaum, *Bloomsbury Group*, 389–95. As Rosenbaum points out (388), Leavis granted "a real and fine distinction" to Forster's fiction but considered his criticism marred by the impact of Bloomsbury. For T. S. Eliot's appreciation of Marie Lloyd, see Peter Ackroyd, *T. S. Eliot: A Life* (New York: Simon and Schuster, 1984), 105, 145; for Evelyn Waugh's appreciation of the music hall, see Martin Stannard, *Evelyn Waugh: The Early Years, 1903–1939* (New York: Norton, 1987), 448.

7. For Keynes's bluntly stated faith in the bourgeois intelligentsia, see section 4 on politics in his *Essays in Persuasion* (1931; reprint, New York: Norton, 1963).

9. The Narrator

1. The Vintage edition reads "adventures past."

2. Forster, *Aspects*, 79, 78.

3. Ibid, 78–79.

4. I ignore in this brief comparison the complexity of Conrad's deployment of point of view (or points of view) in *Heart of Darkness*: besides Marlow the speaker, there is the anonymous "I" figure aboard the *Nellie* who writes down Marlow's tale; he too, however, is a dramatized figure internal to the story's world.

5. Elizabeth Laughland, "Gesturing toward an open space," 252, 259.

6. Wayne Booth, *The Rhetoric of Fiction (Chicago: University of Chicago Press, 1961), chap. 3.*

7. D. H. Lawrence, *The Complete Short Stories*, vol. 1 (New York: Viking, 1967), 274–75.

8. F. R. Leavis, "E. M. Forster," in Bradbury, *Forster: A Collection of Critical Essays*, 42; K. W. Gransden, *E. M. Forster* (Edinburgh: Oliver and Boyd, 1962), 58–59; Widdowson, *Fiction as History*, 87–90.

9. Kenneth Graham, *Indirections of the Novel: James, Conrad, and Forster* (Cambridge: Cambridge University Press, 1988), 162–68.

10. Gransden, *Forster*, 59.

11. Lest these references seemed strained, I should note that Forster himself refers to Drayton's "incomparable poem." Drayton, the narrator tells us, if he were to write today, "would sing the nymphs of Hertfordshire as indeterminate of feature, with hair obfuscated by the London smoke. Their eyes would be sad, and averted from their fate towards the Northern flats, their leader not Isis or Sabrina, but the slowly flowing Lea. No glory of raiment would be theirs, no urgency of dance; but they would be real nymphs" (206).

12. Daniel Defoe, *A Tour through the Whole Island of Great Britain*, vol. 2, ed. G. D. H. Cole and D. C. Browning, (London: Dent, 1974), 8.

13. Martin J. Wiener, *English Culture and the Decline of the Industrial Spirit, 1850–1980* (Harmondsworth, Eng.: Penguin, 1985).

14. *Selected Poems of Thomas Hardy*, ed. John Crowe Ransom (New York: Macmillan, 1961), 40.

15. "Imperturable British Toryism, viewed . . . across the fields and behind the oaks and beeches . . . is by no means a thing the irresponsible stranger would wish away; it deepens the very colour of the air; it may be said to be the style of the landscape." Henry James, *English Hours* (New York: Weidenfeld & Nicolson, 1989), 142.

16. Philip Gardner, "E. M. Forster and 'The Possession of England'," *Modern Language Quarterly* 42, no. 2 (1981): 170.

17. I am indebted here to Elizabeth Barrett's argument in her "The Advance beyond Daintiness."

18. Cobbett repeatedly describes London as a "wen" or "infernal wen" in his *Rural Rides* (London: Cobbett, 1830).

10. Only Connect . . .

1. Trilling, *Forster*, 22.

2. Thomas Mulvey, "A Paraphrase of Nietzsche in Forster's *Howards End*," *Notes and Queries* 19, No. 2 (February 1972): 52, refers to the Nietzschean context of Helen's "nightmare theory" and proposes also that

Notes and References

Henry Wilcox's obviously discredited views on male and female roles in chapter 31 ("Man is for war, woman for the recreation of the warrior" [255]) derive from *Thus Spake Zarathustra* (1883–92).

3. Stallybrass, *Manuscripts of "Howards End,"* xii.

4. Gardner, *Critical Heritage*, 130.

5. F. R. Leavis, "E. M. Forster," in Bradbury, *Forster: A Collection of Critical Essays*, 35.

6. John Colmer, "Marriage and Personal Relations in Forster's Fiction," in Herz and Martin, *Centenary Revaluations*, 113.

7. P. N. Furbank, "The Philosophy of E. M. Forster," in Herz and Martin, *Centenary Revaluations*, 46.

8. *Aspects*, 132.

9. Trilling, *Forster*, 129.

10. Bill Maxwell, "Florida Today: A Plundered Garden of Eden," *Gainesville Sun*, 11 August 1990.

Bibliography

Primary Sources

Fiction

The standard edition of Forster's writings, published by Edward Arnold (London), is the multivolume *Abinger Edition of E.M. Forster*, which includes:

Where Angels Fear to Tread (vol. 1). Edited by Oliver Stallybrass. 1975.

The Longest Journey (vol. 2). Edited by Elizabeth Heine. 1984.

A Room with a View (vol. 3). Edited by Oliver Stallybrass. 1977.

Howards End (vol. 4). Edited by Oliver Stallybrass. 1973. The editor's introduction discusses the circumstances of the novel's composition, thematic motifs, and reception. The appendix provides Forster's account of Rooksnest, his childhood home and the model for Howards End. The notes annotate the novel's unfamiliar allusions. The paperback edition (Harmondsworth, Eng.: Penguin, 1987) reproduces, in addition to the text, the editor's introduction, notes, and the Rooksnest Memoir. The Vintage edition (New York: Random House, 1989) is used in this study.

The Manuscripts of "Howards End" (vol. 4a). Correlated with Forster's final version by Oliver Stallybrass. 1973. Indispensable to the serious student of the novel.

A Passage to India (vol. 6). Edited by Oliver Stallybrass. 1978.

The Life to Come and Other Stories (vol. 8). Edited by Oliver Stallybrass. 1972.

Two Cheers for Democracy (vol. 11). Edited by Oliver Stallybrass. 1972.

Aspects of the Novel and Related Writings (vol. 12). Edited by Oliver Stallybrass. 1974.

Goldsworthy Lowes Dickinson and Related Writings (vol. 13). Edited by Oliver Stallybrass. 1973.

Selected Bibliography

Other Fiction

The Collected Tales of E. M. Forster. New York: Modern Library, 1968.

Maurice: A Novel. New York: Norton, 1971.

Howards End. Edited by Oliver Stallybrass. Harmondsworth, Middlesex, Eng.: Penguin, 1987.

Howards End. New York: Random House, 1989.

Other Nonfiction

Aspects of the Novel. New York: Harcourt Brace, 1955.

Marianne Thornton, 1797–1887: A Domestic Biography. London: Edward Arnold, 1956.

Abinger Harvest. New York: Harcourt Brace, 1964.

Two Cheers for Democracy. New York: Harcourt Brace, 1965.

Commonplace Book. Edited by Philip Gardner. Aldershot, Eng.: Wildwood House, 1988.

Letters

Selected Letters of E. M. Forster, 1879–1920, vol. 1. Edited by Mary Lago and P. N. Furbank. Cambridge, Mass.: Belknap Press of Harvard University Press, 1983.

Selected Letters of E. M. Forster, 1921–1970, vol. 2. Edited by Mary Lago and P. N. Furbank. Cambridge, Mass.: Belknap Press of Harvard University Press, 1985.

Secondary Sources

Forster's Literary Milieu

Howards End is one of a number of works treating "the condition of England" (to cite the title of C. F. G. Masterman's sociological study of 1909) in the period. The following novels (and Shaw's play) are a representative sample of works that bear on *Howards End*. Editions and publishers are not listed; dates are of those of first publication.

Butler, Samuel. *The Way of All Flesh* (1903). A novel of filial revolt against the Victorian patriarchy.

Conrad, Joseph. *The Heart of Darkness* (1902). A profound critique of European imperialism and the "hollow men" who upheld it.

Galsworthy, John. *The Country House* (1907). Describes the life of rural gentry challenged by the urban plutocracy.

James, Henry. *The Spoils of Poynton* (1897). A novel about good and bad heirs, and right and wrong uses of property.

Lawrence, D. H. *The White Peacock* (1911). A story of failed relationships, set in an idyllic English countryside.

London, Jack. *The People of the Abyss* (1903). A fictional account of the squalor, poverty, and ill health of the "very poor" in the East End of London.

Shaw, George Bernard. *Major Barbara* (1905). Contains, in Andrew Undershaft, the weapons manufacturer, a forceful spokesman for laissez-faire capitalist practices.

Sturgis, Howard Overing. *Belchamber* (1904). A fictional critique of class attitudes in a country-house setting.

Wells, H. G. *Tono-Bungay* (1909). A novel setting the order and beauty of Bladesover (a country house) against the energy and corruption of private enterprise.

Bibliographies

Kirkpatrick, B. J. *A Bibliography of E. M. Forster*, 2d ed. Oxford: Clarendon Press, 1985. Includes information on Forster's books, pamphlets, contributions to books and pamphlets, contributions to periodicals and newspapers, translations of his works, audiovisual material, and manuscripts. Specifies the English and American editions of *Howards End* up to 1983 and 1982, respectively, and provides the number of copies sold and the price per copy.

McDowell, Frederick P. W. *E. M. Forster: An Annotated Bibliography of Writings about Him*. De Kalb: Northern Illinois University Press, 1976. Contains helpful summaries and evaluations of 1,913 books and articles on Forster up to 1975. Regrettably, this monumental work lacks a topical index.

Gardner, Philip. *E. M. Forster: The Critical Heritage*. London: Routledge and Kegan Paul, 1973. Useful and interesting collection of early reviews and criticism.

Biographies

Furbank, P. N. *E. M. Forster: A Life*. New York: Harcourt Brace, 1981. One-volume paperback edition of the authorized and standard biography, first published in two volumes in 1977 and 1978.

Selected Bibliography

King, Francis. *E. M. Forster*. London: Thames and Hudson, 1978. Concise account with excellent photographs.

Critical Studies—Books

John B. Beer. *The Achievement of E. M. Forster*. New York: Barnes and Noble, 1962. Chapter 1 interestingly sets Forster's fiction in relation to romantic poetry and music.

Bradbury, Malcolm, ed. *Forster: A Collection of Critical Essays*. Englewood Cliffs, N.J.: Prentice-Hall, 1966. A standard collection including important essays on Forster by I. A. Richards, Peter Burra, F. R. Leavis, and Bradbury's own essay on *Howards End*.

Cavaliero, Glen. *A Reading of E. M. Forster*. Totowa, N.J.: Rowman and Littlefield, 1979. Good account of *Howards End* in the context of other fiction of the time.

Colmer, John. *E. M. Forster: The Personal Voice*. London: Routledge and Kegan Paul, 1975. Fine discussion of *Howards End* in the context of other "condition of England" works.

Crews, Frederick C. *E. M. Forster: The Perils of Humanism*. Princeton: Princeton University Press, 1962. Important and incisive study that argues the thesis implied in the title. Very good on Forster's political background.

Das, G. K. and John Beer, eds. *E. M. Forster: A Human Exploration, Centenary Essays*. London: Macmillan, 1979.

Finkelstein, Bonnie B. *Forster's Women: Eternal Differences*. New York: Columbia University Press, 1975. Sympathetic consideration of Forster's female characters, especially Margaret.

Gillie, Christopher. *A Preface to Forster*. New York: Longman, 1983. Readable and informed treatment of Forster's novels and their social and intellectual contexts.

Herz, Judith Scherer, and Robert K. Martin, eds. *E. M. Forster: Centenary Revaluations*. London: Macmillan, 1982. Contains important essays on or relating to *Howards End* by established Forster scholars, including Wilfred Stone, P. N. Furbank, S. P. Rosenbaum, and Frederick P. W. McDowell.

McDowell, Frederick P. W. *E. M. Forster*, rev. ed. Boston: Twayne, 1982. A sane, factually rich interpretation.

Martin, John Sayre. *E. M. Forster: The Endless Journey*. Cambridge: Cambridge University Press, 1976. Fine exploration of sea and river imagery in *Howards End*.

Page, Norman. *E. M. Forster*. New York: St. Martin's, 1987. Good reading of *Howards End* with deft attention to symbols (e.g., hay and motorcar).

Stallybrass, Oliver, ed. *Aspects of E. M. Forster*. New York: Harcourt Brace,

1969. A collection of genial essays and recollections written for Forster's ninetieth birthday.

Stone, Wilfred. *The Cave and the Mountain: A Study of E. M. Forster*. London: Oxford University Press, 1966. Major scholarly study of Forster's religious background (the Clapham Sect), intellectual background (particularly his debt to Coleridge and Bentham), and the Cambridge Apostles (particularly the influence of G. E. Moore). Like Crews, Stone is critical of *Howards End*.

Summers, Claude J. *E. M. Forster*. New York: Ungar, 1983. Notable for its sensible criticism of the critics of Forster's homosexual writings.

Thomson, George H. *The Fiction of E. M. Forster*. Detroit: Wayne State University Press, 1967. Contains good "archetypal" interpretations.

Trilling, Lionel. *E. M. Forster*. New York: New Directions, [1943] 1964. A major study by a major critic, who himself belonged to the liberal tradition. Trilling proclaimed *Howards End* as Forster's masterpiece.

Twentieth-Century Literature 31, nos. 2–3 (1985). A rich issue devoted to Forster, with articles on *Howards End* by Philip Gardner, Pat C. Hoy II, Mary Pinkerton, and Andrea Weatherhead. Also a useful survey of the Forster papers in the King's College Archives by Michael Halls, the then "modern" archivist.

Widdowson, Peter. *E. M. Forster's "Howards End": Fiction as History*. London: Chatto and Windus/Sussex University Press, 1977. Important "cultural materialist" critique of Forster's liberalism; *Howards End* considered as a document in the crisis of liberalism in the twentieth century. Excellent comparison of the novel with C. F. G. Masterman's *The Condition of England*.

Wilde, Alan, ed. *Critical Essays on E. M. Forster*. Boston: G. K. Hall, 1985. The editor's introduction has a good, balanced review of recent Forster criticism.

Critical Studies—Articles and Chapters in Books

Colmer, John. "Marriage and Personal Relations in Forster's Fiction." In Herz and Martin, *Centenary Revaluations*. Excellent discussion of the tension between sexual preference and fictional conventions in Forster's work.

Delany, Paul. " 'Islands of Money': Rentier Culture in E. M. Forster's *Howards End*." *English Literature in Transition, 1880–1920* 31, no. 3 (1988): 285–96. Fine treatment of the parasitism of imperial investment.'

Gardner, Philip. "E. M. Forster and 'the Possession of England.' " *Modern Language Quarterly* 42, no. 2 (1981): 166–83. Sympathetic to Forster's eulogies of rural England.

Selected Bibliography

Hardy, John Edward. "*Howards End*: The Sacred Center." In *Man in the Modern Novel*. Seattle: University of Washington Press, 1964. Affirmative reading of novel's ending.

Langland, Elizabeth. "Gesturing toward an Open Space: Gender, Form, and Language in E. M. Forster's *Howards End*." In *Out of Bounds: Male Writers and Gender(ed) Criticism*. Edited by Laura Claridge and Elizabeth Langland. Amherst: University of Massachusetts Press, 1990. Excellent account of the sexual politics of *Howards End*.

Rosecrance, Barbara. "The Postponement of England's Decline: *Howards End*." In *Edwardian and Georgian Fiction: 1880–1914*. Edited by Harold Bloom. New York: Chelsea House, 1990. Another critique of Forster's liberalism, with a good treatment of the narrator.

Rivenberg, Paul R. "The Role of the Essayist-Commentator in *Howards End*." In Herz and Martin, *Centenary Revaluations*. Interesting analysis of the novel's discourse.

Smith, H. A. "Forster's Humanism and the Nineteenth Century." In Bradbury, *Forster*. Excellent history-of-ideas article.

Stape, J. H. "Leonard's 'Fatal Forgotten Umbrella': Sex and the Manuscript Revision to *Howards End*." *Journal of Modern Literature* 9, no. 1 (1981–82): 123–32. Shows how a study of the manuscripts can illuminate Forster's intentions.

Stone, Wilfred. "E. M. Forster's Subversive Individualism." In Herz and Martin, *Centenary Revaluations*. A good rebuttal of those who dismiss Forster's politics.

Wyatt-Brown, Anne M. "*Howards End*: Celibacy and Stalemate." *Psychohistory Review*, 12, no. 1 (1983): 26–33. Relates *Howards End* to conflicts in Forster's early childhood.

Period Studies

Colls, Robert, and Philip Dodd, eds. *Englishness: Politics and Culture, 1880–1920*. London: Croom Helm, 1986. Contains excellent articles on English culture, politics, literature, music, and the cult of the rural.

Ensor, R. C. K. *England 1870–1914*. Oxford: Clarendon Press, 1936. A standard, still authoritative history.

Hynes, Samuel. *The Edwardian Turn of Mind*. Princeton: Princeton University Press, 1968. A classic work of literary history.

Rose, Jonathan. *The Edwardian Temperament, 1895–1919*. Athens: Ohio University Press, 1986. Incisive and broad-ranging work of intellectual history.

Rosenbaum, S. P., ed. *The Bloomsbury Group*. Toronto: University of Toronto Press, 1975. An invaluable collection of memoirs and commentaries that describes the group of which Forster was a somewhat shadowy member.

Stubbs, Patricia. *Women and Fiction: Feminism and the Novel 1880–1920.* New York: Barnes and Noble, 1979. Though unsympathetic to Forster's view of women, this is a pioneering study.

Index

Admiralty, 4
Altman, Denis, 20
Aristotelian criticism, 27–28, 33, 40, 41–42, 111, 135
Annan, Noel, 17
Arnim-Schlagenthin, Elizabeth, Countess von, 32
Arnold, Matthew, 17, 18, 32, 50, 73, 86, *107–8*, 128, 137; *Culture and Anarchy*, 108
Athenaeum, 75
Austen, Jane, 9, 15, 35, 58–59, 75, 78, 96, 104, 120, 134, 138; *Emma*, 63, 145n13; *Mansfield Park*, 54, 58, 64; *Pride and Prejudice*, 10; *Sense and Sensibility*, 42, 67, 84, 99, 145n4

Bachelard, Gaston, 61–62, 73; on house image, 61
Bakhtin, Mikhail M., 28, 33
Barthes, Roland, 27–28, 100, 134
Beer, John, 17
Beethoven, Ludwig van, 43, 117, 118, 124; Fifth Symphony, 35–40, 71; Seventh Symphony, 36; Ninth Symphony, 73
Bell, Clive, 18, 35; *Art*, 33
Bell, Vanessa, 18
Bennett, Arnold, 3, 13–14, 15
Bentham, Jeremy, 5, 18, 32, 70, 103

Blake, William, 17, 148–49n3
Bloomsbury Group, 18, 33–36, 47, 106, 109, 149n6
Booth, Wayne, 116
Borrow, George, 108
Brooke, Rupert: "The Old Vicarage, Grantchester," 127
Burke, Edmund, 70, 87, 117; *Reflections on the Revolution in France*, 70; *Letter to a Noble Lord*, 70
Butler, Samuel, 120

Cambridge, 18, 102, 117
Camden, William: *Britannia*, 124
Carpenter, Edward, 80, 89; *The Intermediate Sex*, 148n11
Cavaliero, Glenn, 19
Chamberlain, Joseph, 5; and tariff reform, 5–6. *See also* liberal imperialism, *Howards End*
Chaucer, Geoffrey, 128
Clapham Sect, 6, 18, 141n6
Cobbett, William, 128
Coleridge, Samuel Taylor, 17, 18, 107, 137
Colmer, John, 19, 135
Conrad, Joseph, 3, 13, 39, 83, 112; *Heart of Darkness*; 92, *114–15*, 118, 132
Crews, Frederick C., 19, 46, 135; *E. M. Forster: The Perils of Humanism*, 17, 18, 22, 74

Darwin, Charles, 85
Debussy, Claude, 9, 36, 104
Defoe, Daniel: *Tour through the Whole Island of Great Britain*, 125
Dialogism, 33, 111, 121, 137. *See also* Bakhtin
Dickens, Charles: *Hard Times*, 32
Dickinson, Goldsworthy Lowes, 6, 18
Drayton, Michael: *Poly-Olbion*, 124, 150n11

Edward VII (king of England), 3
Edwardian period (1901–10), 3–7, 8–10, 18, 22, 42–43, 51, 73, 76, 89
Eichenbaum, Boris (Russian formalist), 27–28
Elgar, Edward: *Pomp and Circumstance*, 4; *Coronation Ode*, 4
Eliot, George, 15; *Felix Holt*, 58
Eliot, T. S., 73, 107; *Burnt Norton*, 73; *The Waste Land*, 128
Ensor, R. C. K., 68
Epstein, Joseph, 20

Farrer, Reginald: *My Rock Garden*, 67; *Alpines and Bog Plants*, 67
Faulkner, William, *Sound and the Fury, The*, 66
Finkelstein, Bonnie: *Forster's Women*, 20
Fisher, Admiral John, 126
Flaubert, Gustave, 112
Florida, North, 138–39
Ford, Ford Madox, 112; *The Good Soldier*, 117–18
Forster, E. M.: amateur musicologist, 38; attitude to money, 77, 129–30; attitude to plot, 27–28, 46–47; (*see also* Aristotelian criticism); BBC broadcast conversation, 102; belief in comradeship, 89; capitalism, critique of, 59, 64–65, 72; childhood at Rooksnest, 7, 59–61; concern for the environment, 10, 128–29, 131; concern for the poor, 5–6, 50, 77–78, 115–16, 120; conservatism, 59, 61–62, 70, 73–74; criticism of Bentham's utilitarianism, 32, 70, 103 (*see also* Bentham); departure from West Hackhurst, 61–62; distrust of technology, 10, 59, 69, *131–32* (*see also* motorcar, *Howards End*); ear for speech and dialogue, 9, 94, *97–101*; feminist criticism of, 20–21; friendship with Bob Buckingham, 102, 109, 130; frustrated dramatist, 96–97; homosexuality, 13, 20, *79–80*, 134–35, 143n19, 147–48n6; liberalism, 5–7, 11, 16, 21, 74, 91; love of railway stations, 120–21; novelist of manners, 9, 74, 75, 79, 134; onomastic decorum, 30–32, 53; public schools, critique of, 9, 66, 80, *99–100*, 117; tutor at Nassenheide, Pomerania, 32; relation to Bloomsbury Group (*see* Bloomsbury Group); relation to Clapham Sect, 5–6 (*see also* Clapham Sect); relation to modern fiction, 112–15, 130, 137 (*see also* Conrad; Ford; James; Woolf); relation to romantic tradition, 17–18; representation of time, 42; respect for rural community, 10, 45–46, 70, 139; rivalry with Woolf, 15,

Index

20, 142n7; voice, 106, 149n5; references to Germany and Germans, 30–32, 78, 97–98, 126, 134; satire of intellectuals, 100–101

PROSE
"Anonymity: An Enquiry," 33
"Art for Art's Sake," 33
Aspects of the Novel, 15, 33, 41, 54, 76, 88, 90, 112, 135
"Challenge of Our Time, The," 7, 34, 62
Commonplace Book, 19, 27
"Conversations in the Train," 102
Deceased Wife's Husband, The, 97
Heart of Bosnia, The, 97
Hill of Devi, 17
Howards End: character typology, 54, 78, chronology, 42–45; critical reception, 12–23; descriptions (ekphrasis), 48, 62, 123–28; epigraph ("Only Connect . . ."), 8, 84, 131–39, 141n1; historical context, 3–7; manuscript drafts, 31, 50, 51, 67, 92, 94, 95 (illus.), 108, 122, 126, 148–49n3; meals ("tea-tabling"), 9–10, 47–48, 100–102, 103, 110 (*see also* Isherwood, Christopher); metonymic technique, 10, 58, 69, 73; mimesis (and diegesis), 36–38, 47, 48, 94, 110–11, 134; narrator's plurality, 48–49, 117–18; plot (and story), 41–47; point of view, 113–19, 137; reader's plurality, 118–19, 137; rhythm and tempo, 47–51, 134; *style indirect libre*, 36–39, 87, 93,

113, 116; use of Cockney, 50; use of French, 49–50; use of marriage plot, 11, 54–55, 74, 79–80, 87, 89–90; use of pronouns, 119–23; "work" and "text," 27–30, 54, 82, 134

CHARACTERS
Avery, Miss, 45, 51, 71–73, 77, 91, 98, 139
Bast, Jacky, 49–50, 78, 88–89, 94, 97, 107, 122
Bast, Leonard, 38, 43–46, 50–51, 75–77, 93–94, 102–9, 117, 120, 122–23, 132–33
Brace, Hamar, 52–54, 78
Edser, Lady, 99
Förstmeister, Herr, 134
Fussell, Colonel, 99
Howard, Tom, 64, 71
Mansbridge, Mr., 90
Mosebach, Fräulein (Frau Architect Liesecke), 35, 97–98
Munt, Mrs. (Aunt Juley), 4, 35, 68, 78, 83, 88, 97–98, 104, 113
Schlegel, Ernst, 30–32, 51
Schlegel, Helen, 20, 29–31, 35–40, 42–55, 62–63, 69, 73–74, 75–76, 82–84, 104–6, 108, 125–26, 132
Schlegel, Margaret, 4, 9–10, 11, 20, 21, 35–36, 42–55, 60, 74, 75–82, 83–93, 85–93, 96–101, 104–6, 108–11, 116, 121, 123–26, 129, 132
Schlegel, Tibby, 10, 35, 36, 76, 80–81, 96, 148n8
Schlegels, 45–46, 91–92, 97, 104, 126
Wilcox, Charles, 4, 9, 31, 44, 45, 51–54, 66, 68–70, 79, 83, 86, 92, 100, 103, 115, 133
Wilcox, Mrs. Charles (Dolly), 72, 79, 98–99, 113

Wilcox, Evie, 10, 66–67, 68, 77, 99
Wilcox, Henry, 43–50, 63–65, 76–77, 81–91, 91–92, 96, 99, 109–10, 114, 134
Wilcox, Mrs. (neé Ruth Howard), 43, 45, 61–63, 65, 69–71, 83, 100–102, 124, 135–36
Wilcox, Paul, 36, 78, 79, 82–83, 92, 103
Wilcoxes, 45–46, 53, 82, 91–92, 97, 103, 108, 114, 126, 132, 138
POLITICAL REFERENCES
Fabianism, 5, 10, 22; laissez-faire, 5, 10, 50, 85, 107; liberal imperialists, 4–5, 45, 49–50, 51, 64, 87, 94, 99–100; liberalism, 4–5, 7, 11, 13, 21, 50, 59, 64, 74, 91, 109, 110, 130; social Darwinism, 11, 50, 85, 93, 117; socialism, 6, 110, 130; tariff reform, 4
SYMBOLISM
Ahab, Ananias, and Jezebel (puppies), 67; Books, 51, 91; Dutch bible, 4–5; garage, 63, 67–68; house, 45–46, 58–59, 62–65, 139; hay, 10, 65, 71, 73, 88; motorcar, 5, 9, 67–69, 83, 86, 113, 117, 128–29, 138; sword, 51, 107; telegrams, 4, 83–84; vine, 60, 63, 71; wych-elm tree, 46, 59, 60, 63, 67–68, 71, 89
THEMES
Culture, 50–51, 104, 106–110, 113, 117, 136–37, 148n9; death, 54, 117, 130, 132–33; friendship of Schlegel sisters, 54, 74, 75, 79, 135; games and sports, 9, 65–67, 69, 73, 134, 138; gardens (rockeries), 10, 67, 69, 72–73, 134; house and garden improvements, 59, 63,

64–65, 74; money, 9, 76–78, 104, 109, 129–30, 132; sexuality, 81–82, 83–84, 87, 89–92; suburbia, 5, 54, 138–139
WORKS
Letters, 19
Life to Come, The, 19, 20; locked journal, 132, 145n4, 147n6
Longest Journey, The, 20, 80, 120, 135
Marianne Thornton, 17, 62
Maurice, 19, 20, 80, 135; memoir of writing career, 47
"Not Listening to Music," 36; notebook journal, 79–80, 89, 102–03, 131, 147n6
Passage to India, A, 13, 18, 19, 20, 22, 80, 99, 101
"Raison d'Etre of Criticism in the Arts, The," 33
Rede lecture on Virginia Woolf, 15
Rooksnest memoir, 59–61
Room with a View, A, 19, 28–29
"Story of a Panic, The," 129
Two Cheers for Democracy, 17
West Hackhurst memoir, 62
Where Angels Fear to Tread, 41, 80, 120

Fry, Roger, 18, 33, 35
Furbank, P. N., 19, 135

Galsworthy, John, 3, 13, 15, 22, 66
Games. See Forster, sports and games
Gardner, Philip, 127; Critical Heritage, 12
Gemeinschaft (and Gesellschaft), 45, 52, 69, 138, 145–46n6
Gesellschaft. See Gemeinschaft
Gillie, Christopher, 19
Gladstone, William Ewart, 4

Index

Gibbon, Lewis Grassic, 23
Goldsmith, Oliver: *The Vicar of Wakefield*, 133
Golf. *See also* Forster, sports and games; Faulkner
Graham, Kenneth, 124, 126
Grandsen, K. W., 124
Grant, Duncan: *Portrait of James Strachey*, 81

Hardy, Thomas, 42; "Channel Firing," 127
Heteroglossia, 33, 111. *See also* Bakhtin
Holme, Constance, 22
Hynes, Samuel, 20

Independent Review, 6
Irish nationalists, 3–4
Isherwood, Christopher, 48, 146n10
Ivory, James, 19

James, Henry, 15, 27–28, 34–35, 53, 58, 112–113, 134; *The Ambassadors*, 41, 112; *English Hours*, 127, 150n15
Jefferies, Richard, 108
Joyce, James, 84, 112

Keats, John, 16, 128
Kermode, Frank, 24, 136
Keynes, John Maynard, 18, 106, 109
Kirkpatrick, B. J.: *Bibliography of E. M. Forster*, 12

Labour party, 6, 62
Langland, Elizabeth, 21, 116
Lavery, Sir John, 3
Lawrence, D. H., 22, 23, 69, 80, 84, 92, 106, 119, 134; "The Christening," 119–120
Lean, David, 19
Leavis, F. R., 16, 107, 124, 134
Liberal party, 4–7

Lloyd George, David, 6, 45, 68; "people's budget," 6, 68
London, Jack: *People of the Abyss*, 5
Lubbock, Percy: *Craft of Fiction, The*, 112
Lucas, F. L., 108
Lukács, Georg, 78

McDowell, Frederick P. W.: *Annotated Bibliography*, 12
McTaggart, J. M. E., 18
Magdalen College, 10
Malthus, Thomas, 85, 103
Mansfield, Katherine, 14, 15
Marcus, Jane, 20
Martin, John Sayre, 19
Masterman, C. F. G.: *Condition of England, The*, 5, 21, 22, 123
Mauron, Charles, 13
Maxwell, Bill, 138–39
Meredith, George, 108
Merrill, George, 80
Mill, James, 5
Mill, John Stuart, 17, 133
Milton, John, 17, 128
Monet, Claude, 9, 36, 104
Moore, G.E., 18
Morris, William: *News from Nowhere*, 58

Nation, The (London), 46
Nietzsche, Friedrich, 133; *Beyond Good and Evil*, 133; *Thus Spake Zarathustra*, 150–51n2

Old Testament, 10, 67
Oxford, 81, 96–97, 117
Ozick, Cynthia, 20

Page, Norman, 19
Plato: *Republic*, 110
Putnam's (publisher), 29

Queen's Hall, 35, 43, 104

Reid, Forest, 46, 136
Ricardo, David, 5, 85
Richards, I. A., 16
Richardson, Samuel, 29; *Sir Charles Grandison*, 58
Rivenburg, Paul, 34
Rowntree, Seebohm, 5
Ruskin, John, 18
Russell, Bertrand, 18, 106

Sargent, John Singer, 3
Sassoon, Siegfried, 100
Schiller: *Ode to Joy*, 73
Scott, Walter, 58–59, 78, 146–47n9
Scott-James, R. A., 13, 14
Shakespeare, William, 70, 128; *Richard II*, 126
Shaw, George Bernard, 5, 22; *Major Barbara*, 92
Shelley, Percy Bysshe, 17, 89; *Prometheus Unbound*, 89; *Adonais*, 89
Shklovsky, Viktor (Russian formalist), 27–28
Simpsons in the Strand, 9–10, 48, 50, 66, 86, 93, 99, 109–10
Sitwell, Sir George, 67
Smith, Adam, 5, 85, 103
Smith, H. A., 17
Smollett, Tobias: *Humphry Smollett*, 64–65, 72
Stevenson, Robert Louis, 108
South African ("Boer") War, 4
Sports. *See* Sports and games, Forster
Stallybrass, Oliver, 19, 67, 134
Stendhal, 78
Stone, Wilfred: *Cave and the Mountain*, 17, 18–19, 33, 46, 71, 74, 135; "E. M. Forster's Subversive Individualism," 143n19

Strachey, Giles Lytton, 18, 96; *Eminent Victorians*, 65
Stubbs, Patricia, 20
Suffragettes, 4
Summers, Claude, 19

Taff Vale Case, 4
Tolstoy, Leo, 78, 113
Trilling: *E. M. Forster*, 16–17, 18, 20, 132, 136–37
Trollope, Anthony, 28; *Barchester Towers*, 115

Ulster unionists, 4

Wagner, Richard, 9, 104: *Tannhäuser*, 104, 108
Waugh, Evelyn, 107; *Brideshead Revisited*, 58, 59
War office, 4
Webb, Sidney, and Beatrice, 5
Wedd, Nathaniel, 18
Wells, H. G., 3, 15, 22, 60, 133; *Tono Bungay*, 60; "Machine Stops, The," 131
Widdowson, Peter: *"Howards End": Fiction as History*, 21–24, 124, 137; "A Literature for England," 22
Wiener, Martin, 125
Wilde, Alan, 19
Wilde, Oscar, 96; *The Importance of Being Earnest*, 97
Williams, Raymond, 23
Woolf, Virginia, 15, 16, 20, 29, 76, 112; *Atlantic Monthly* article on Forster, 15; *Mr. Bennet and Mrs Brown*, 15; *Mrs. Dalloway*, 29; *Nation* review, 15; *Room of One's Own*, 76; *Three Guineas*, 76. *See also* Woolf, Forster
Wordsworth, William, 87, 107; Preface to *Lyrical Ballads*, 107

The Author

Alistair M. Duckworth received an M.A. degree (1958) from the University of Edinburgh and, after a short service commission in the Royal Navy, M.A. (1964) and Ph.D. (1967) degrees from the Johns Hopkins University. Author of *The Improvement of the Estate: A Study of Jane Austen's Novels* (1971) and (with David Streatfield) of *Landscape in the Gardens and the Literature of Eighteenth-Century England* (1981), he has written and lectured extensively on English fiction and the relations between literature and landscape. He serves on the editorial boards of *Eighteenth-Century Fiction* and the *South Atlantic Review* and has been a Guggenheim fellow (1977–78) and a visiting fellow at Magdalen College, Oxford (1989). In 1990 he received a university award for outstanding undergraduate teaching at the University of Florida, Gainesville, where he is a professor of English.

DATE DUE

JUL 0 2 2009			
GAYLORD			PRINTED IN U.S.A.